Dispatches From Puerto Nowhere

AN AMERICAN STORY OF
ASSIMILATION AND ERASURE

Robert Lopez

Two Dollar Radio
Books too loud to Ignore

Two Dollar Radio
Books too loud to Ignore

WHO WE ARE Two Dollar Radio is a family-run outfit dedicated to reaffirming the cultural and artistic spirit of the publishing industry. We aim to do this by presenting bold works of literary merit, each book, individually and collectively, providing a sonic progression that we believe to be too loud to ignore.

TwoDollarRadio.com

Proudly based in
Columbus OHIO

 @TwoDollarRadio

 @TwoDollarRadio

 /TwoDollarRadio

Printed in Canada

Love the **PLANET?**
So do we.

Printed on Rolland Enviro.
This paper contains 100% post-consumer fiber, is manufactured using renewable energy - Biogas and processed chlorine free.

 100%   **PCF**   BIO GAS ENERGY   PERMANENT

SOME RECOMMENDED LOCATIONS FOR READING:
Pretty much anywhere because books are portable and the perfect technology!

AUTHOR PHOTO→
Jenny Pommiss

PHOTO→
Robert Lopez

COVER PHOTO→
Karim MANJRA
on Unsplash

Editor: Eric Obenauf. Copy Editor: Asia Atuah.

Portions of this book previously appeared in different forms in *The Sun*, *New England Review*, *Longreads*, *Hobart*, *The Rupture*, and *Los Angeles Review of Books*.

Two Dollar Radio acknowledges that the land where we live and work is the contemporary territory of multiple Indigenous Nations.

Dispatches From Puerto Nowhere

What I don't know about my family is almost everything.

I don't know when or why my grandfather left Puerto Rico, although I can make assumptions about jobs and opportunity and the nebulous *better way of life* that can be applied to countless immigrants.

I don't know anything about his family, if he had brothers or sisters, who his parents were or what they did for a living. I don't know if he left anyone behind on the island to come to Brooklyn.

I never asked questions and no one in my family told those kinds of stories.

I know less about my grandmother. I do know she was born in New York City, but I know nothing of her parents. I remember hearing that one was from Spain and the other from Cuba, but I don't know which was which or why they immigrated to the U.S.

Nothing was passed down, not the language, not the food or music, or the family history.

Everything was erased.

I don't know what my father knew about his heritage. I don't know if he ever met his grandparents or knew anything about them. I don't know if he ever went to Puerto Rico or heard stories about his father's life there.

The story my father told our family was that he understood his parents' Spanish but would respond in English when he was a kid growing up in Brooklyn.

I never saw any evidence that my father understood Spanish.

An immigrant is a person who has come to live permanently in a foreign country.

If you stand in exactly the right spot in Brooklyn Heights with a good pair of binoculars you can't come close to seeing Puerto Rico.

The same is true if you stand on high ground in Miami, if there is high ground in Miami.

What in this life is permanent when everything is foreign?

I pity the poor immigrant when his gladness comes to pass, said Bob Dylan.

Cultural assimilation is when individuals or groups of differing ethnic heritage are absorbed into the dominant culture of a society. The process involves taking on the traits of the dominant culture to such a degree that the assimilating group becomes socially indistinguishable from other members of the society.

Here in the United States, they are whitewashed.

It's rare for a minority group to replace its previous cultural practices completely, particularly during the last 50 years, but before that it happened all the time.

Puerto Rico has been part of the United States since Woodrow Wilson signed the Jones-Shafroth Act in 1917.

But Puerto Rico has never really been part of the United States and no one thinks of Puerto Rico as part of the United States, so I think of my grandfather as an immigrant.

I go back and forth with what I've lost through erasure and what I've gained by assimilation and what it all means.

The back and forth is like a tennis rally and how different shots behave on the court. Mario's flat backhand will rush through the air and stay low, whereas the topspin Teddy puts on his forehand will have the ball kangaroo past shoulder level. Wayne's backhand slice skids off the ground and eats you up if you're not ready for it.

In Brooklyn I live in the American melting pot exemplified by the diverse tennis community of which I'm a part. Most everyone has a history or at least a mythology, the stories we tell each other and ourselves, idealized narratives that we can talk about during changeovers and water breaks.

Even I play the game, but it's a hollowed-out mythology when I tell it and almost entirely a fiction. I sometimes tell them that my grandfather was a housepainter or guitarist for Tito Puente, that he toured the country and Latin America until it was time to get married and raise children, but I can also say that he was a longshoreman or boxer who had two or three families and was an absentee father and grandfather, which was why my own father never learned Spanish and neither did I.

My grandmother never taught me any Spanish but said I should learn in school. The example she provided to underscore the importance of learning Spanish had to do with her experience riding a subway and overhearing two men planning some sort of crime. She found a cop on the platform and ratted the would-be criminals out and this was why I should learn the language.

My grandmother was earnest in this advice. There was no other reason to learn or speak Spanish.

Dispatch From The Unaffiliated

My name is Robert Lopez and I look like my name is Robert Lopez.

This has only recently occurred to me, that I look Latino.

Before this realization I'd never spent time thinking about how others perceive me. I grew up surrounded by white people and never thought of myself as *other*. My father never said that we're Puerto Rican so this means some people will consider us second-class citizens and we'll be subjected to scorn and prejudice. No one ever told me that teachers and coaches and employers and policemen might treat me differently.

I didn't think of myself as white, per se, so perhaps the most apt categorization would be… unaffiliated.

That's me, Robert Lopez, Unaffiliated.

I had to ask friends a pointed question when I started writing this book, what do you see when you look at me? and they all said that I look Latino, that they don't think of me as white and never have.

A tennis partner from years ago named Jason, a Black Panamanian, expressed surprise when I told him I was Puerto Rican. He said he thought I was Black.

I'd heard this before. A close friend named Shelly relayed an anecdote about a party we'd attended and how years later someone else at that party referenced the Black man Shelly was with. Shelly didn't know what this woman was talking about until she realized the woman meant me.

Playing pickup basketball in the early '90s, a tough Irish football player who was also good at roundball said he was going to "smother my Black ass" as he volunteered to guard me.

I lit him up that day.

Dispatch From 1970s Long Island

The first time someone called me a spic was during recess or after school in the playground or in the park across the street from my house on Long Island. I was in shirtsleeves and it was hot or I had on a heavy winter coat with a ski hat and gloves and boots because it had snowed overnight and we could see our breath in the frigid winter cold.

I like the thought of the word *spic* hanging frozen in the air, the vapors of which are exhaled and linger for an unnatural period of time, like in a cartoon, until they disappear.

That's how I've experienced most of what's happened to me, from childhood on, as a series of vapors, exhalations and disappearances.

These vapors go back even further. Maybe the starting point was 1904, the year U.S. engineers began work on the Panama Canal and New York City unveiled its first underground subway line.

That same year, over a thousand miles away on an island in the Caribbean Sea, my grandfather, Sixto Lopez, was born.

Maybe his mother gave birth to him on a Sunday during a turbulent spring rainstorm. The dirt road through town was washed out and impassable and that's why the one doctor they knew of couldn't assist with the delivery.

It was Sixto's *abuelita* who wiped the sweat from his mother's brow, extolled her to push through the pain and gently received him as he writhed and wailed and took his first shallow breaths, glowing pink and gelatinous with blood and afterbirth.

He took his final shallow breaths in a bathtub in Brooklyn in November 1987.

I was a sophomore in high school, my sister an eighth grader. When we got home from school our mother's car was in the driveway, which was unusual. Normally she'd have been at work, but her presence didn't set off any sort of alarm when I first saw her and I wasn't concerned or worried.

She broke the news to us in the foyer as soon as we entered the house and I remember trying to cry as an appropriate response. I knew that was what you were supposed to do when your grandfather died. I'd seen it on television and in the movies, though I hadn't known anyone who'd died up to that point in my life, so I had no practical experience.

About two or three seconds into this futile attempt at weeping I stopped, realizing it was ridiculous.

Dispatch From A Winter Tableau

One probably wouldn't imagine a winter tableau replete with snowdrifts and icicles as a realistic setting where one person calls another a spic for the first time.

I've always liked winter best and still do. I like the cold. I like that night starts early and lasts forever. I like walking to the super-market without working up a sweat.

I wonder how many half Ricans prefer winter to summer.

Back when children wore snowsuits come December and Jan-uary, the ones that had the mittens sewn into the sleeves, the winters were majestic all over New York. There were blizzards every other weekend and drifts would bury the cars parked in the streets and the trees lining the sidewalks. It seemed as if we would never see the cars again and if school ever did reopen we'd have to use wooden tennis rackets as makeshift snowshoes and tramp through the snow to get there.

My mother and father took photographs of the cars, of my sis-ter and me, all buried and content and whited out on our lawn outside of our Levitt house in the middle of a particularly con-servative and culturally bankrupt part of the country known as Long Island.

The Long Island of the '70s and '80s was a different sort of conservatism than what we see today. Back then it was about money and greed and racism and law and order and the military.

Maybe it wasn't entirely different.

Perhaps the differences lay in a particular kind of small-mindedness, a suburban ignorance when it came to matters of sex, drugs, freedom of expression, individuality. There wasn't anything Christian about this conservatism, not overtly, but it was somewhat puritanical and devoid of any meaningful culture.

My sister and I would go out to the backyard and build snow forts. We did this in matching snowsuits, designed to keep us safe and dry and warm, which were bulky and ridiculous and didn't allow for any sort of athletic maneuver. You couldn't fight in them, for instance, but you could build a fort and after the fort was built you could do almost anything, such as build another fort right next to it.

I have no memory of what, if anything, we did inside the forts.

The first time someone called me a spic I was six or nine or eleven years old.

The last time someone called me a spic was probably in high school and most likely a term of endearment.

Getting called a spic didn't bother me more than, say, getting called *hyperactive* by my childhood friend, Joey, who lived across the street.

I felt obligated to chase Joey down after he called me hyperactive one day in the park. His evasive maneuvers were ineffective and I caught up to him and threw one or two haymakers that put him on the ground.

We were maybe seven or eight and Joey was a head taller than me.

Joey called me hyperactive because I always wanted to keep playing hockey or baseball or football or basketball when everyone else wanted to quit and go hang out on the playground.

If anyone called me any kind of name when I was a kid I was likely to throw down, because I was both hyperactive and fearless back then. Same was true if someone made a mother or father or sister joke, regardless of the content.

Spic didn't cut deeper, but it had a provocative power I couldn't quite understand.

I don't think my sister was ever called a spic, regardless of the weather.

I don't think girls were called spics in the 1980s. Maybe they never were.

Dispatch From Stony Brook University's
Department Of Corrections

This past week in class one of my grad students mentioned that she was called a spic in Brockton, Massachusetts, in the 2010s.

Dispatch From The Moon

My father came home later that evening, having gone to Brooklyn to help his mother earlier in the day. I don't know what he did there, but I imagine it had to involve making arrangements, visiting a funeral parlor, maybe cleaning up the mess left behind when someone dies in the house. I was nervous about seeing him, as I didn't know what I should do or say and I didn't know how my father would react to losing his father.

My father was always the strongest man I'd ever known, but I didn't know if that strength would extend to grief. His arms were the size of my legs then and even his wrists were thick and muscled. It'd been only recently that I could keep up with him in a footrace even though I was fast. And he was fearless, always the first to stand up to trouble or rush to someone's defense, particularly his family's. But I didn't know if something like that mattered. It seemed unrelated, beside the point.

I didn't know how any of it was supposed to work.

We rushed over to console him when he came through the door and he was stoic and strong, as always. Then he walked into the kitchen and hung his head over the oil burner that was tucked into a wall that separated the kitchen from the living room. It was the posture of someone crying, maybe for the first time in his life. My father was almost out of eyeshot of his children and I went into the living room to give him even more privacy.

I don't know if I did it for him or me.

As I type this sentence I am 47 years old, the same age as my father when his father died.

All of it seems unbelievable and as far away as the moon.

My grandfather had been suffering from prostate cancer that probably occurred and reoccurred and by the end of his life he had grown thin and frail. I can't recall if it was that night or sometime in the next week, during the wake and funeral, that my father said if the paramedics had attempted to resuscitate him his chest would've caved in.

Or that they did try to resuscitate him and his chest did cave in.

No iron spike can pierce a human heart as icily as a period in the right place, said Isaac Babel.

I had no emotional connection to my grandfather and I can't say that I felt any sort of affection for him, neither while he was alive nor after he'd died. Like most children I suppose I was somewhat afraid of older people, regardless of relation. His thick accent also kept me at arm's length, as I had a hard time understanding him.

I had even less affection for my grandmother, his wife.

For years I thought this indicated there was something wrong with me, but I never spent that much time thinking about it.

Maybe this was a byproduct of assimilation. Maybe if they'd insisted my father speak Spanish and his children speak Spanish and spoke Spanish to all of us and talked about Puerto Rico and what it's like to live there as a second-class U.S. citizen and educated us about traditions and customs and food and music, then something like a bond could've been forged.

Maybe we could've made *tostones* and *maduros* on *el Día de Reyes* while listening to José Feliciano singing "Feliz Navidad."

Or maybe nothing would've fostered a connection with them.

Dispatch From Krakow

For years I've been misquoting the late Polish poet Czesław Miłosz without knowing that Miłosz is the one I've been misquoting. I've done this, I'm sure, because I heard someone else misquote Miłosz. I'm pretty sure this person did so without attribution, as well.

How far back it goes is unknowable, of course, but it's akin to a literary telephone game that is entirely without consequence or the least bit interesting.

What I've been saying is this: When a writer is born into a family it's the end of the family.

I preface this statement with the inarguable, A writer once said.

I used to think Flannery O'Connor said this about writers and families, as it sounds like something she would've said.

It isn't scholarly or academic to say *a writer once said*, but it gets the point across to students. I trot this misquote out whenever I'm trying to get students to risk more on the page, whenever I see them tap dance around potentially interesting and dangerous material. I use the Miłosz quote to give them license to let it fly, to destroy themselves and their families.

I employ any number of quotes and misquotes when I teach fiction and nonfiction writing to students. Babel, Hemingway,

Faulkner, Chekhov, Didion, Pritchett, Hannah, Shakespeare, O'Connor, Morrison, Borges, Stengel, Berra, Ray Charles, A writer, etc.

The actual quote attributed to Miłosz is: When a writer is born into a family the family is finished.

I like the misquote better.

There's a finality to the misquote that feels apocalyptic, whereas the actual quote sounds softer. One can finish a coffee table or a deck. One lover can ask another, *Did you finish*, and it would be considerate. A diamond is finished as are countless other precious gemstones and earthly items.

A family finished can mean they've attained the pinnacle of human achievement. No reason to go any further, to go forth and continue with this mindless multiplying, for we have birthed a writer.

Dispatch From One Way of Looking At It

I am not here to destroy or finish my family.

The Lopez side of my family, in most ways one can measure, was finished long ago.

Dispatch From The Caribbean

Puerto Rico is that tiny island in the Caribbean where the beaches are immaculate and the women are beautiful and the food is free and everyone makes love and drinks rum and plays baseball all day long and into the night.

Puerto Rico is that tiny island in the Caribbean that is split between two countries and on the other side is Haiti and there are earthquakes and hurricanes and poverty and corruption and dictators and juntas and movie stars adopting orphans.

Puerto Rico is that tiny island in the Caribbean where it's the third or fourth world and there's no running water or electricity and only state-run television and radio and there's no internet but everyone can read and write and all the cars are from the 1950s and they make the best cigars and had a dictator who lived and ruled over everyone for 114 years.

Puerto Rico is that tiny island in the Caribbean where they speak French or Dutch or English and invented reggae and practice voodoo and they're always bracing for hurricanes and marauding Europeans and everyone is beautiful and they make love and play baseball and drink rum all day long and into the night.

Dispatch From 407 Washington Ave

I decided to watch the Puerto Rican Day Parade and then I decided to make a day of it. I put on some Tito Puente and made a complicated sandwich that included sliced tomatoes, avocado, and sprouts.

I hoped I would learn or feel something as I watched the Puerto Rican Day Parade on television in Brooklyn while the Puerto Ricans paraded up Fifth Avenue in Manhattan.

At the same time in Paris, Rafael Nadal of Mallorca, Spain, was winning the French Open for the 12th time in his distinguished career. Nadal is a supernatural force on clay, a slower surface which suits his unrelenting style, where he retrieves ball after ball and sends it back into his opponent's court with incredible depth and spin until he decides he's had enough of such foolishness and flattens out a screaming down-the-line winner to end the point, the game, the set, the match, the championship.

Nadal was on NBC and the parade was on ABC and I went back and forth so I wouldn't miss anything.

Much have I traveled in the realms of gold, said John Keats.

Dispatch From Highland Park

The day before the parade I played tennis with Jorge, Can, and Sunil in Highland Park because we couldn't get a court at Fort Greene Park and then we couldn't get on the court at the Cage in Bed-Stuy. There was some sort of event for kids wearing green tee shirts and holding miniature tennis rackets.

One must wake very early on the weekends, 6:30 or so, and stand in a long line with other tennis crazies to secure a court at Fort Greene Park. It's entirely objectionable and uncivilized. None of the four of us were willing to do this. I am never willing, but others freely volunteer on a rotating basis and I often take full advantage of their insanity.

After the selfish children at the Cage body-blocked us from playing, I drove our quorum of doubles players to Highland Park in my girlfriend's car, a small red Fiat you can lift off the ground with minimal effort. Jorge is Guatemalan, Can Turkish, Sunil British by way of India. Jorge called it a clown car, as he was the last to get in, sitting in the front passenger side, legs folded up under his chin.

A coalition rainbow in an Italian clown car. Where's Fellini when you need him.

We saw dozens of Puerto Rican flags on cars and on poles and in storefronts on the drive through Bushwick to get to Highland.

No one mentioned any of the flags, not the Turk, not the Brit, or the Guatemalan. So when I said we saw them I'm not sure that's true. I saw them.

This was the 62nd National Puerto Rican Day Parade but the first one I watched on television.

It's obvious I've never attended a Puerto Rican Day Parade, nor did my father, I'm pretty sure. Like me he was never much of a Puerto Rican, didn't claim or display any pride whatsoever in being one.

I've never felt a compulsion to parade around as a flag-waving member of the PR tribe because why would I.

To be fair, I've never been ashamed of being Puerto Rican, either.

Dispatch From As Long As I'm Here

I've never felt a compulsion to parade around for any reason.

Dispatch From The End Of The Line

The Lopez side of my family ended on its own and it had nothing to do with any writer.

I suppose while I am still living and while my sister is likewise this particular Lopez family has not quite ended, not technically. But as my sister took her husband's name and I have no children presently and will not father any in the future, this Lopez line will die with me.

Dispatch From Puerto Nowhere

According to a Morning Consult-*New York Times* poll conducted in 2017 in the wake of Hurricane Maria, almost half of Americans didn't realize Puerto Rico is a U.S. territory.

Puerto Ricans living on the island cannot vote for president and do not have congressional representation.

One must fill out an international slip to mail a package from the mainland to Puerto Rico.

Since 1898 Congress has debated 101 bills related to citizenship in Puerto Rico and enacted 11 overlapping citizenship laws, with all kinds of crazy provisions and caveats, including the law prohibiting foreign-flagged ships from delivering cargo to Puerto Rico.

To this day it isn't clear if Puerto Rican citizens enjoy the same equal protection guarantees under the 14th Amendment.

Puerto Ricans pay the same payroll taxes as mainland Americans, but don't get the same Social Security or Medicaid benefits.

Puerto Rico is the land that democratic theory forgot, said Luis Fuentes-Rohwer, Indiana University law professor.

Dispatch From The Land Of Opportunity

I'm trying to rethink all that's happened to me and determine how my ethnicity might've played a part.

I don't know what else my last name has cost me. Maybe jobs, opportunities, relationships.

I think about what I may've gained, too. That maybe I get paid to read and teach at universities in part because my name is Lopez.

Dispatch From The Political Extreme

In January 2022, federal prosecutors filed seditious conspiracy charges against the leader of the far-right organization the Oath Keepers and ten other individuals for their role in the January 6, 2021, attack on the U.S. Capitol. It was one of the very rare instances in which this law, aimed at protecting the government from attacks, had been applied in U.S. history.

However rare these charges are levied, they were brought against Puerto Ricans throughout the 20th century.

Including when four armed Puerto Rican nationalists opened fire on members of the U.S. Congress in 1954.

Also when two Puerto Rican nationalists tried to assassinate President Truman in 1950.

According to María Luisa Paúl in *The Washington Post*, this militancy began in the 1930s, three decades after the United States acquired Puerto Rico from Spain, when Pedro Albizu Campos, a graduate from Harvard University, became president of the Puerto Rican Nationalist Party. He believed that the island's colonial situation "caused the material and moral misery of his people" and that "the only way to redeem this besieged group was through insurrection."

Dispatch From Mayagüez

Sixto turns 12 tomorrow and his mother is making *pernil* and *mofongo* and *arroz con gandules* and for dessert there will be sliced pineapple. He doesn't know that his mother has been saving for a guitar and will present it to him after supper when they are alone and the rest of the household has gone to bed.

He wants to try playing the guitar that night, but she tells him to wait till morning so as not to wake anyone.

The next day Sixto rises early and rushes over to the guitar. Within minutes he is picking out chord shapes and making music, as if he's been playing for years. He wonders if it's the guitar itself, that maybe the fret board has the power to direct the player's fingers into the proper positions. But then he hands the instrument to his older brother, Orlando, who immediately breaks a string and then bangs on its body as though it were a drum.

Dispatch From Half A Fragment

Lopez is the 12th most common surname in the country, with about 874,500 people sharing the name, according to the 2010 U.S. census.

I don't know any of these Lopezes personally, though I've met one or two in passing, had conversations, studied expressions, and listened to words, what was between and behind them. I've seen the disappointment and disapproval when another Lopez learns that I don't speak Spanish.

If there was any hint of kinship it was once or twice removed and long ago, metaphorical at best, and perhaps only resided in the imagination.

Sixto Lopez, my grandfather, was born in 1904 in Mayagüez, Puerto Rico, and died in November 1987 in Brooklyn, New York. In between he lived and worked in Brooklyn, fathered and raised three children, one dying before maturity.

He was Popop to my sister and me, not Grandpa or Grandfather and never Abuelo or Abuelito.

I think I remember seeing a photo of my father's older sister, the one who died. The photo was black and white and the girl was very young, between three and ten, and she had on a frilly dress. She may've been holding hands with my grandmother.

I don't know what her name was, what she died from or when.

I do not come from a line of storytellers and apparently I was never curious enough to ask.

It's possible I was curious enough to ask but no one wanted to talk about it. It's possible I was told these basic facts and have since forgotten them. I don't think this is likely, though. There is so much I don't know about the Lopez side of the family that I'd have to have suffered some sort of brain injury to forget so much of it.

Fragments are the only forms I trust, said Donald Barthelme.

I'm not sure what constitutes a fragment when it comes to what I know about my family.

What's less than half a fragment? What's part of a shard?

The family was already in critical condition before the Lopezes started getting killed off.

Families are comprised of narratives, like history and novels. If there are no family stories then the family ceases to exist.

Joan Didion said we tell stories in order to live. We could amend it to say in order to survive, as well.

Dispatch From Fort Greene Park

My sister called when I was on the court, playing against Mario Aguilar. I could hear the phone ringing inside my bag, but we were in the middle of a baseline rally and Mario was running me around with his flat two-handed shots from both sides. I didn't stop to answer. He held his service game at love and after three or four deuces I followed suit. It was during the changeover that I saw the text message, that something wasn't right with Mom, how she'd gone to work that morning but couldn't remember getting there, couldn't recall anything about her day. Christine said she was going to take her to the hospital.

I apologized to Mario, told him what was going on and that I had to go, may've even said *lo siento* because I can at least pronounce some of the words like a native.

Playing against Mario is a challenge but it has little to do with the unorthodoxy of his groundstrokes and nothing to do with family emergencies. You can never relax while playing against him is the problem. Every shot must have a purpose because he destroys every single short ball with impunity, and good luck sending him an otherwise neutral ball deep down the middle of the court because he'll find some crazy angle for a winner from back there, as well. He is also relentless and indefatigable, getting to every cross-court forehand or down-the-line backhand or perfectly disguised drop shot, always making you hit an extra ball or three. He's exhausting.

And whenever I hear him break into Spanish with someone like Jorge or Noë or Avril it feels like I should be playing somewhere else, somewhere with the other imposters.

But none of that mattered because I was on a train to New Jersey and I couldn't let my brain get ahead of me and I didn't want to think about what might be going horribly wrong with the wiring inside my mother's brain.

I didn't think about tennis on the train, but I can't remember what I did to distract myself. For most of the past ten years, tennis has been the ultimate distraction. It's soul-saving therapy four or five times a week, as there is nothing like running around and smacking the hell out of a ball. It's the best way I know to kill time.

Thoreau said, As if you could kill time without injuring eternity.

Eternity is unassailable, that's how.

But human brains and bodies are too easily assailed and while I was on the train, trying to kill time, my mother was in a hospital, maybe having a stroke or some other brain-related catastrophe. I didn't want to think about how this might change her life, change everything. I certainly didn't want to think the worst, so I tried not to think about anything, which I've never been good at. I tried meditation once or twice and the whole time kept thinking about ways to handle Kenny's left-handed serve spinning out wide in the ad court or how next time I'll come to the net more often against Mario to shorten the rallies and I'll hit two first serves because you have to take chances when you play someone like him.

Maybe I brought a book or magazine or I played Scrabble on my phone.

By the time I arrived at the hospital, though, Mom was alert and in good spirits and I was relieved and free to think about how life might not have to change after all. They were running tests and we still didn't know what was wrong, but I could afford to be hopeful. I could think about spending the night, having dinner with the family, and then heading back to Brooklyn for my scheduled hit with Saj at 5 the following afternoon, provided my mother was given a clean bill.

The problem was she still couldn't remember anything about that day and kept on repeating herself as though she had no short-term memory at all.

Dispatch From Where I Belong

Now when it snows I stay inside. Maybe I look out the window for signs of life, but I wait for the city to plow the streets and for the building superintendents to shovel the sidewalks before I venture out into the world unless it is necessary, unless I have no choice and it's about food or the possibility of tennis or sex.

I never play in the snow, stopped all that around the age of eight. I hear stories of grown people sledding in the park or cross-country skiing after a blizzard, building snow structures and the like.

A woman I once dated expressed consternation when I didn't throw a snowball at her after she pelted me with one while we were out walking one winter's day. She accused me of having no fun.

Now I like it best when I go on Stony Brook University's website and they say that all classes are canceled.

I don't do anything special or especially productive with this unexpected day off and it isn't as if I don't like my job, but it still feels like a get-out-of-jail-free card.

I'll stay inside for days until order is restored, until it stops snowing and the wind isn't a constant assault.

I have no problem with the cold, but snow and wind are another story.

I do the same thing during a heat wave unless it is necessary I play tennis. Most often we wait until the sun begins to hide behind the trees so we can play in shadows.

I prefer playing in cooler temperatures and if I had to pick between freezing in 35 degrees and sweltering in 90, it's an easy choice.

Maybe this is a betrayal of my ancestry or maybe it's a natural evolutionary response, embracing this harsh new environment way up in the North Country.

Regardless, all of this amounts to staying safe, cocooned and comfortable, and away from the outside world, away from danger.

The world is none of my business sometimes.

Inside I have countless books and cable television and a vast library of music, two air conditioners, two guitars, and there are even people to bring me food whenever I'm hungry. All I have to do is sign on and order up, tip the delivery person two or three or four dollars.

The world changed during the pandemic but it fell right in line with my not wanting to leave the house, so it wasn't much of an adjustment.

Inside a snow fort on Long Island, inside an apartment building in Clinton Hill, Brooklyn, there is safety or the illusion of such.

There is safety from efforts that started 80 years ago in other parts of Brooklyn and the Bronx, when my parents' parents were desperate to have their children accepted as Americans. Insisting the children speak English at home and everywhere else, no discernible trace of an accent.

Dispatch From This One Will Last A Lifetime

I've never attended any parade, not even when the Rangers won the Stanley Cup in 1994. I'll never blemish this record of conscientious absence, even if my niece or nephew were to win the US Open, cure cancer, and get elected and inaugurated as president all on the same day.

I watched the Rangers parading down the Canyon of Heroes that day in June 1994 from the safety of my living room. It was like being there without having to be there, which is almost always preferable, and in this case saved me from being subjected to the company of a million drunk and rowdy ruffians.

That same day in 1994 O.J. Simpson paraded around the freeways of Los Angeles in the white Ford Bronco, evading police in the slowest car chase in history.

I watched part of that show from a strip club in Farmingdale on Long Island with one of my best friends growing up, Ron Chin.

The strippers stopped stripping and the patrons stopped ogling the strippers so everyone could watch the circus unfold on national television. Everyone wanted to see where O.J. was going and what he would do when he got there. His longtime friend and chauffeur on this day, A.C., said he had a gun to his head. I'm sure a lot of people wanted O.J. to blow his brains out right there in front of the cameras.

We all love a spectacle.

Meanwhile, mayor Rudolph Giuliani was presenting Rangers playoff hero Brian Leetch with a key to New York City.

How many Puerto Ricans' favorite sport is ice hockey, particularly those born in Brooklyn in 1940 and one generation removed from the island. How many of those Puerto Ricans bequeath such love for Canada's national game to their son born 31 years later.

I'm sure the paradegoers had to line up early to attend the spectacle, both for the Puerto Ricans and the Rangers.

People were on the side of the freeways and on overpasses rooting O.J. along on his tour of Los Angeles. Some held makeshift signs imploring O.J. to keep on running.

Dispatch From You Think You've Got Problems

My mother had a transient ischemic attack (TIA) about 20 years ago, which is a mini stroke, but life didn't change for her or our family as a result. She'd had some tingling and numbness in one of her arms, but nothing that alarming, nothing disastrous. There were no other symptoms, no repercussions, and no actual damage. She's been taking blood thinners and blood pressure medication since the TIA and regularly visits a cardiologist.

I've had what I self-diagnosed as carpal tunnel syndrome for years. My hands tingle and go numb all the time. In fact, they are never not tingling and all the typing and tennis and fingerpicking make it impossible for the nerves to ever heal or regenerate. I even had to forgo tennis and guitar for six weeks a few years ago when I lost all strength in my right hand and couldn't make a fist.

I've learned to live with this, but when I felt the same tingling in my feet I thought I might have multiple sclerosis or ALS. I actually went to a doctor, which is unusual for me because I rarely visit doctors and don't trust them.

I think they did a blood test and sent me for an MRI, but I lasted only three seconds inside that sarcophagus before I pushed the panic button and got the hell out of there. I figured I'd find out sooner or later if I had MS and everything would resolve itself when I die anyway.

What I do have is any number of troubling parasomnias. I wake up thinking I'm dead and I can't breathe. Sometimes I fly out of bed, desperate for air. It takes about five long seconds to regain my senses, realize what's happening. Sleep apnea is one possibility, but the symptomology doesn't add up and the same is true of night terrors, which typically last much longer than what I experience.

Lately, I've had neck issues and this has me waking up thinking I'm having a stroke. It's not just my hands that tingle anymore, but my whole arm from the shoulder down. There is pain near the elbow, wrist, biceps. When it runs down my left arm I think it's a heart attack.

I wait for something worse to happen and after a few minutes I tell myself not today and maybe I'm fine and that lots of people are insane like this.

Dispatch From Saint Barnabas Medical Center
In Livingston, New Jersey

Years earlier, my mother had collapsed on December 18, 2008, her 61st birthday, while attending my nephew Jake's first-grade Christmas pageant. Four days later she had an aortic valve replacement. She'd known for years that she'd eventually need this operation, but the way it was framed to her by doctors was, *One day you'll climb the stairs and be out of breath and this is when we'll do it.*

It took her quite a while to recover from the operation, which we'd tried to reassure her was as routine as a haircut. Of course, we meant from the surgeon's perspective, but that's not how our comfort was delivered or interpreted. When we saw her in recovery the first thing she said was, still groggy from the anesthesia, this was no haircut.

I grew up with the fear that something awful would happen to my father, and eventually it did when he died suddenly of cardiac arrhythmia at 56. But for whatever reason I was confident that my mother would be fine, that she'd pull through this surgery and go on like before.

I wasn't quite as confident years later as I rode the train to New Jersey after playing tennis with Mario, perhaps attributable to the difference between a 61-year-old woman with no prior health problems and a 70-year-old with a five-inch scar starting at the base of her throat and running down the middle of her chest. But there was also the knowledge that things go wrong with these fallible human bodies and it gets more inevitable the longer you stay at the fair.

After a battery of tests, however, over the course of a long day and night, the doctors found nothing amiss with my mother's heart or brain and she was discharged the next day.

We had visions of having to sell her house since we wouldn't want her to climb stairs, changes in diet, and all kinds of other ramifications that we couldn't imagine but figured would be part of our lives. This is what we talked about at dinner while our mother was spending the night in the hospital. We all sounded stoic and strong and pragmatic as hell.

The next day we learned that what my mother had experienced is called transient global amnesia, which is defined by the Mayo Clinic as a sudden, temporary episode of memory loss that can't be attributed to a more common neurological condition, such as epilepsy or stroke. During an episode of transient global amnesia, your recall of recent events simply vanishes, so you can't remember where you are or how you got there.

There's nothing to be done about this, nothing to treat, nothing to do to prevent it.

It's something that happens.

Dispatch From 1918

Sixto practices guitar all hours day and night and it doesn't matter if his mother tells him to go outside and play ball with his friends or if his brother, Orlando, is making a nuisance of himself or if his mother's dog is doing likewise.

Besides, he's not sure how he feels about his mother's dog or his brother or any of his friends. He's not even sure he has friends.

Once he left home in the middle of the night without telling anyone where he was going. He took his guitar and camped out in the hills above Mayagüez for a week. He played and played until the blood from the ripped-open calluses on his fingers dripped all over the neck and fretboard. When he returned home he looked like a madman.

Dispatch From Clinton Hill

I wish I could speak Spanish to Jorge, whom I sometimes call Jorgito because others call him El Capitan due to his penchant for telling people what to do. I like cutting him down to size, though I'm not sure he or anyone else is aware that this is what I'm doing. Regardless, he and I have a good rapport, joke easily and often, and laugh a lot on the court.

I hear him speaking Spanish to Mario and Noë and Carlos and Avril, even Pierre because he's French but has worked in restaurants his whole life. Mauro, from Italy, also speaks Spanish, and has owned and operated restaurants.

I'm not in that club, the Spanish club, the multilingual club.

But I can trade wicked cross-court forehands with Mauro and can return Noë's big first serve, so there's always that.

I never felt like an outsider or imposter when I heard the kitchen staff speaking Spanish in the restaurants I worked in when I was younger, though that's exactly what I was. Probably I was impervious to such feelings because I was young and naïve and had lived a sheltered life.

I was a waiter at a slew of restaurants, including an Italian eatery, for a dozen or so years. Every kitchen was populated with Latinos speaking mile-a-minute Spanish. But for all I cared they might as well have been Turkish or French or Chinese. They were none of my business.

But it's different now with my tennis friends and as I move around the world as a rootless, ersatz Puerto Rican nearing age 50.

Dispatch From Almost Everywhere

In my girlfriend Jenny's bathroom there was a mirror inside a mirror. I never looked at my reflection in the inside mirror. Instead my focus was on locating whatever medicine or first-aid item I might've needed from the cabinet as quickly as possible so I could close it.

I sometimes caught a glimpse of myself between the shelving.

I don't like looking at myself in a mirror. Whenever I do I'm reminded that I'm getting older fast.

I'd stocked her medicine cabinet with allergy medication, Advil, over-the-counter sleep aids, antacids, vitamins, and aspirin.

I haven't taken aspirin since I was a child, but an ex-girlfriend, whose father is a cardiologist, suggested I keep aspirin on hand in case of the heart attack I imagine having all the time.

Yesterday I had a breakfast of vitamins and Advil and played tennis with a man named Cary Ng, who works as a freelance graphic designer and has taught at Parsons School of Design. During our match Cary told me he grew up in Puerto Rico and went to an American-style prep school in San Juan, where he was taught in English but also took classes in Spanish. He told me he speaks Spanish, though not fluently, as he spoke Cantonese at home. But he speaks enough Spanish to watch *Narcos* without subtitles and he speaks Spanish when he travels abroad.

I admired him for being multilingual because I always admire this ability and when I told him my story like I've done a million times before—My father didn't speak Spanish at all and thus we never spoke it at home and my mother is Italian and this factor and that caveat and such and so—he said he knew plenty like me, including his wife.

I probably said that I'd like to learn to speak Spanish, but I know I missed my chance and it's over for me.

I'd need Spanish to be an over-the-counter pill I could take out of the medicine cabinet and swallow once a day or as needed.

Had I been born to Chinese parents who then moved me as a child to Puerto Rico in the 1980s I probably would've learned Spanish, too.

I do have the desire to speak Spanish, but that desire exists in a vacuum and is worthless. It's akin to saying I wish I were taller or wish that I'd picked up tennis when I was a kid.

I'm not at all willing to put in the countless hours of practice and study to achieve even nominal fluency. There's too much to do and too much tennis to play.

Learning the language now won't change that I was born in Brooklyn to an assimilated Puerto Rican who didn't speak Spanish and later moved his family out to Milquetoast, Long Island, as countless others did in the early 1970s.

It won't change that my father was also born in Brooklyn, in 1940, the golden age of assimilation. But his stories about growing up had to do with playing stickball and street hockey with his friends. Maybe all Latinos played stickball in the city, but hockey was probably another story. It seems like particular proof of assimilation or whitewashing and perhaps to some, proof of progress.

My grandfather, Sixto, spoke Spanish with my grandmother and broken English with his grandchildren until he died at 83 after a bout or two with cancer.

I only assume my grandfather fled Puerto Rico in his 20s out of deductive reasoning. Maybe he was in his 30s, given that his firstborn, my late Aunt Gloria, was born around 1937.

I assume my grandparents insisted their children speak English all the time with everyone everywhere. Despite my father's assertion, I'm not sure I believe that my grandparents spoke to him in Spanish and he'd reply in English.

Of course, the language is only part of what's been lost, maybe the least of it. There's also food, music, any sort of belief system, customs and mores, but most of all, history.

What I don't know about my family is almost everything.

A permanent amnesia, local and global.

Dispatch From Center Court

My sister and I, long out of the snow forts on Long Island, are victims of this amnesia.

On the court you can empty your mind and concentrate solely on the ball. This is what it always comes down to: see the ball and hit it. This is how so many Latin baseball players approach hitting, observing the maxim, You can't walk off the island.

But matters of identity and history and culture are all-the-time complex and can cripple a person, or in my case, cause a certain discomfort I can't quite articulate.

This is the *how can you miss what you never had* trope. I can say I'm Puerto Rican and no one can refute it, but I don't know what it's like to feel Puerto Rican. I don't know what it's like to see the flag and feel something other than indifference. I don't know what it's like to feel a kinship with those who share the same heritage. It's a greater tragedy than not knowing what it feels like to be six feet tall or born into affluence.

Now I know I look Puerto Rican. I've been asked by any number of Latinos where I'm from and how come I don't speak the language. A Spanish-speaking stranger will speak to me like they assume I'll understand.

That I was born Puerto Rican was happenstance, but that I have no connection to what it means is no accident. My grandparents made conscious decisions and so did my father, as part of the first generation born here in the States.

And none of it bothered me until recently, which is probably why I can't quite put my finger on any of this. I'm still grappling with what I've lost and how I can miss something I've never had.

Dispatch From The Caribbean

In Puerto Rico they let the children play baseball or tennis all day long instead of going to school.

In Puerto Rico there is sweet fruit hanging from every tree and the trees are everywhere.

In Puerto Rico there's no law against speeding, so you can drive 100 miles per hour up and down scenic highways and busy turnpikes, avenues or boulevards, and no one ever gets into an accident.

In Puerto Rico people play music together on street corners and in auditoriums and backyards and you can't go five minutes or half a mile without hearing a woman's beautiful alto voice singing jíbaro folk songs or a tight *cuarteto* playing bolero ballads.

Dispatch From Long Island

In high school some of us took to calling each other by epithets. I don't recall ever addressing anyone this way, but maybe I did or probably I did or surely I did.

I definitely referred to myself that way, as a spic, and thought myself clever to have coined a term, *spicguinea*, to capture the entirety of my ethnic makeup.

In a collection of racial or ethnic epithets, *spic* ranks where? It doesn't sound like an insult, like it can be injurious. Perhaps because it sounds like *slick*, which, like countless other words, can be insulting or a compliment.

Perhaps the word *spic* seems harmless to me because it is mono-syllabic. Other monosyllabic slurs also sound either innocuous or ridiculous… *kike, chink, coon, kraut, mick, shine, spade, spook, wop, yid, zip.*

One does notice on this list of monosyllabic slurs, garnered from Wikipedia's page devoted to ethnic and racial epithets, that there are quite a lot reserved for Black people.

Racists are a creative and prolific people.

Most of the words are ridiculous and some sound worse than others and at the same time there're twigs and rocks so I don't know where that leaves anyone.

None are as taboo or as lacerating or satisfying to say as *cunt*, which is all about the acoustics and has nothing to do with meaning or origin, to my way of thinking.

Fuck works the same way. Aside from its versatility, it is satisfying to say out loud.

Probably both *fuck* and *cunt* are enjoyable to say out loud because of a common Germanic heritage. Perhaps it's about white supremacy over curse words.

I used to describe myself as half Puerto Rican and half Italian and half Cuban and half Spanish. I called it the new math.

Of course, it wasn't true, those percentages. But saying one was a quarter or eighth or some other tiny fraction of anything always felt idiotic to me.

Which is akin to being classified as a quadroon or octoroon, which was also ridiculous and awful.

During American slavery, *quadroon* was used to classify a person as having one-fourth African ancestry with one Black grandparent and three white grandparents.

In Latin America, which has a variety of terms for racial groups, some terms for quadroons were *morisco* or *chino*.

In the '90s I worked at an Italian restaurant on Long Island as a waiter, and like in many restaurants in New York both then and now, Latinos staffed the kitchen. One such line cook was referred to as Chino. That's what everyone called him and that's what I called him. I have no idea what his given name was, perhaps it was Roberto or Jesus.

You can imagine why he was called Chino.

The term *mulatto* was used to designate a person who was biracial, with one pure Black parent and one pure white parent or a person whose parents are both mulatto. In some cases, it was used as a general term, for instance on U.S. census classifications, to refer to all persons of mixed race without regard for proportion of ancestries.

The U.S. government used *quadroon* and *octoroon*, for example, as distinctions in laws regarding rights and restrictions.

The only math I did as a teenager was the calculation of batting averages and earned runs, the probability of drawing to an inside straight, now known as a gutshot straight, which you should never attempt.

Now the only math I do is by increments of 15. 15-love, 30-15, deuce.

My tennis community here in Brooklyn is diverse and glorious. In the past year I've played with Mexicans, Guatemalans, Haitians, Jamaicans, folks from Qatar, Egypt, Nigeria, all manner of Europeans, quite a few Australians and South Americans, Chinese, Japanese, Korean, Indian, and Pakistani, even people from Ohio.

White, Black, brown, color and off-color. All kinds of fractions.

Dispatch From The Maestro

One weekend in December 1919, Sixto plays an impromptu concert at the local cantina with a young Spanish guitarist named Andrés, who has traveled from the Port of Valencia to Puerto Rico to see with his own eyes a prodigy who some claim is the best guitarist in the world.

Sixto has become a mythic figure in musical circles due to a feature article written by Diego Goldstein, a prolific journalist who specializes in what would come to be known as human interest stories. The article, first published in *The Times of London* and subsequently translated and reprinted all over the world, likened Sixto to the prodigious talents of Mozart and Paganini. This intrigued Andrés and moved him to alter his travel plans for the forthcoming South American tour.

Andrés, though 11 years older than Sixto, is in awe of the precocious virtuoso. They play together every day for two weeks. Andrés is particularly impressed by young Sixto's right-hand technique while playing arpeggios and how he manages to transcend technique with every note.

Andrés goes on to become the most acclaimed classical guitarist of the 20th century, but he never stops thinking about the young man who taught him how to be an artist in Puerto Rico.

Eventually Sixto decides he enjoys folk music and begins writing his own songs. He composes mostly in the key of D and likes one chord change in particular—an E into F sharp—and how it sounds like an announcement that resolves into something he can't quite identify or explain.

Years later he realizes that chord change is the sound of a subway car pulling into a station, moments before the doors open and people exit the train.

Dispatch From A Mambo King

I have a few vaporous memories of my grandfather, but nothing that would comprise a compelling narrative and nothing at all definitive.

It would be one thing if I'd never met the man, if he were a ghost or myth. If he'd disappeared one day when my father was a kid, leaving the family to fend for themselves so he could sail around the world or hitchhike from town to town while working dead-end jobs or if he were a grifter orchestrating scam after scam, amassing and losing fortunes, over and again, and had another family or two in other parts of the country, maybe one in California, the other upstate.

Whenever I hear or read about someone describing a father or grandfather like this it seems romantic and enviable.

There's Sixto tending to a garden in a small town outside of San Diego. This is his first day home after a month on the road with Tito Puente, for whom he plays guitar and piano. He tells his much younger wife, Esperanza, that he'll be home for at least a month, but it's not true. In two weeks Esperanza will wake to find him gone and she won't see or hear from him for another two months. Esperanza thinks about leaving him, but he's a good father to Pedro when he's home and he's a good provider and this is what it means to be married to a working musician.

Sixto, still vigorous in his late 50s, on the road, playing "Oye Como Va" night after night.

Dispatch From If I Could I Surely Would

People say I should learn Spanish and maybe I could. Maybe it wouldn't take long. But maybe I'm too old to learn anything new and maybe I'm tired of learning. I learned guitar while in college and I taught myself to write fiction and poetry after graduating, deciding this is what I should do with my life. Around the age of 40 I threw myself into tennis and learned the game backward and sideways and now it's an obsession, like music and literature.

Maybe it would be good for me to learn Spanish, but then what? I would still rag on Jorge about his showboating but in a different language. I would talk to the delivery guys in their own tongue. But I couldn't go on and on about how I'm a Latino that doesn't speak the language and I'd have to stop this scribbling and figure out something else to do.

It's kind of like a vasectomy. I know I should get one; it would be to my benefit as I don't want to father any children, but I'm not getting one, not now, not ever.

Maybe it's not at all like a vasectomy. Maybe it's just another thing I'll never do and the reasons don't matter.

Dispatch From Land That I Love

The reasons didn't matter when I worked in restaurants, either.

Inevitably the kitchen staff would find out my name is Lopez and deride me in a good-natured way for not speaking the language. They would ask me where I was from and when I'd tell them they'd laugh and say *Puertorriqueño*. It felt like an inside joke I wasn't privy to, like somehow Puerto Ricans were lower on the Latino pecking order, but I didn't care. Most of them were from Honduras or El Salvador and spoke a dialect that seemed like it was in a rush to get someplace. It seemed as if they were bored with each sentence they spoke aloud and in a big hurry to get it over with so they could get to the next sentence, which sounded the exact same way. Actually, I couldn't discern when one sentence ended and the next began.

They all had dark complexions and dark hair and eyes and were clearly descendants of the natives of Latin America, the Aztecs and Mayans, amongst many others, the ones whom the Spaniards had raped and pillaged into submission. I felt no connection to them on a primal or blood level because why would I.

When people hate on Mexicans it's the Indians they hate, not Salma Hayek or Carlos Fuentes, though maybe they hate them, too.

I come from a time, and maybe that time is still now, where all Latinos were Mexicans, like all Asians were Chinese.

God Bless American ignorance, it knows no bounds.

Dispatch From Puerto Nowhere

I saw Sixto fairly often until he died in 1987 when I was 16. He was always old, always home. No one in the world moved slower than him, his gait more shuffle than walk, shoes never seeming to break contact with the ground. He was always cooking a meal in the kitchen and eating it slowly in the dining room. I shared some of those meals and afterward watched ballgames with him.

Still, I have no idea who he was.

I don't know if he had any brothers or sisters. I don't know anything about his parents, don't know their names or what they did for a living or if they too were native to Puerto Rico or what. I don't know if he left any family behind on the island, don't know if anyone there ever missed him or wrote letters to him or called him on the telephone. I don't know what he did for a living, though my mother says he was a longshoreman. I'd thought he was a painter, but I'm not sure why. I think I saw him once in a pair of paint-splattered khakis, something like what Jackson Pollock might look like after a day in the studio.

I think he served in the United States Army or Navy, maybe as a cook.

I don't know if he had any political affiliation or a particular ideology. I don't know if he voted for Democrats or Republicans or no one at all.

I don't think I ever met anyone from his family, not even at his funeral.

I think I remember that his American friends called him Eddie.

Apparently Sixto was too much for American tongues.

Dispatch From Give Me A Minute

I'm not sure if this is assimilation, if all this was part of it and this is how other people have experienced it, too. That assimilation has always required that one believed the old country was old and left behind for a reason, and we must never speak of it because we are Americans now, which means we speak perfect English at all times and never Spanish at home or anywhere else and our history is the Revolution and Valley Forge and the Battle of Gettysburg and four score to seven years ago our fathers who art in heaven do highly resolve that these dead should not have died in vain, and to the republic for which it stands one nation under hamburgers and strip malls with peace and injustice for all.

I'd sit in class and hear some social studies teacher say that we won the Revolution, won the Civil War, that we've never lost a war until maybe Vietnam, propaganda like this. They'd talk about slavery and emancipation and the Indians and Thanksgiving and I'd look around the room to see if anyone was swallowing this.

I didn't win the Revolution or the Civil War. I didn't enslave anybody. I didn't steal anyone's land or systematically try to wipe out most of a continent's population.

I only just got here, along with the rest of my family, from smack dab in the middle of the Caribbean Sea, an island called Puerto Nowhere.

Dispatch From I Could've Been A Contender

I remember my father pointing out to Sixto that his fly was open and he replied, Nothing to see.

We were getting ready to leave and make the long drive back to Long Island and Sixto was walking us to the door of his Brooklyn apartment. This was maybe a year or two before Sixto died.

There's still nothing to see 35 years later.

I don't know what my grandfather's life was like when he came to Brooklyn. I don't know if he was ever called a spic.

I didn't know what a longshoreman was until college when I saw Marlon Brando in *On the Waterfront*.

The language didn't make sense to me before or after the movie.

A longshoreman is a person who loads and unloads cargo at a dock or port.

So there's Sixto down at the docks, maybe in Red Hook where the IKEA is today or maybe at the Navy Yard where the giant Wegmans stands, and he's pulling on thick gloves with a cargo hook resting over his shoulder and a cigarette dangling from his mouth. He's talking to the shop steward, a man everyone calls Red, and explaining why he had to call out last week. He'd rather not say anything at all, but he heard about a guy who had his union card pulled after not showing up for two days straight. So Sixto tells Red that his daughter died after a brief illness or after she got hit by a bus and they had a wake and funeral and Red puts a heavy hand on Sixto's shoulder and says, I'm sorry to hear that, Eddie.

Dispatch From Red Hook

I also don't know if my father was ever called a spic, growing up in Red Hook. He never said anything and I never asked.

I had to ask my mother where my father grew up. I didn't know the neighborhood, only knew it was Brooklyn.

I had a conversation once with an older gentleman in the early 2010s somewhere on DeKalb Avenue in Fort Greene. He said that years ago there was no such thing as Prospect Heights, Cobble Hill, Park Slope. He said it was all Brooklyn back then. You were from Brooklyn.

When my mother brought my father around to her large Italian family in the Bronx for the first time, an old uncle named Pete (formerly Pietro) told him, "You live in Brooklyn? What are you gonna do?"

Stevedore is another term for longshoreman, the derivation of which comes from Portugal or Spain, *estivador* or *estibador*.

I never heard stories about Puerto Rico, about Italy, about Cuba or Spain. No one ever said that your great-so-and-so came here in 1908 with 38 cents in their pockets and worked as a longshoreman until they earned enough to buy their own fleet of ships and one day you will inherit this empire.

Maybe it was because everyone still had about that same amount in their pockets, more or less.

Maybe they were ashamed of who and what they were and where they came from. Maybe assimilation for them was like a Black grandmother admonishing her grandchild by saying, Don't act your color.

Maybe they weren't storytellers. Maybe none of them possessed any curiosity about these matters.

Maybe they had bigger concerns like food and rent and keeping everyone healthy and off of the streets.

My mother said Sixto married Delores when she was 16. He was older but no more than 22 or 23.

Dispatch From The Docks

Thousands of immigrants from all over worked as longshore-men in the early 20ᵗʰ century.

I've never had much of an imagination. So I can't imagine immi-grating from one country to another in the hopes of a better life and I can't imagine going to the docks every day and moving cargo on and off ships as a way to achieve such.

From *Divided We Stand* by Bruce Nelson:

> ... Some dockworkers were specialists who handled only one type of cargo—coal heavers, grain shovel-ers, cotton screwmen, lumber handlers, and banana "fiends." They worked in gangs that ranged from four men in lumber and cotton to more than thirty in the case of banana handlers. General longshoremen, who dealt with the wide array of goods that most ships transported, were divided into three groups that constituted a clear but permeable occupational hierarchy. The most skilled men worked on deck, operating winches, rigging gear, and guiding the cargo from one place of rest to another. Then came the hold men, whose ability to stow cargo evenly was vital to a ship's safety. Finally, the dock men loaded and unloaded goods on the pier. Although the dock men began as the lowest stratum of the longshore

hierarchy, the introduction of motorized vehicles and other mechanized equipment on the piers gradually propelled them ahead of their counterparts in the hold. "I worked in the [hold] for ten years before I got outta there," New York longshoreman Roy Saunders recalled in 1989. "That was the dogs. That was the worst. Cold in the wintertime, hot in the summer. They thought the men in the hold was the lowest."

I imagine they put the Puerto Rican down in the hold and maybe he stayed there for a long time and maybe he never got out.

Dispatch From The Lowest

I wouldn't have lasted five minutes.

Dispatch From Amsterdam

Dutch colonists established the village of Roode Hoek in 1636, which was named for its red clay soil and the hook shape of its peninsula that juts into the East River.

Before that the Lenape, an indigenous people of what would become New York, Delaware, New Jersey, and Pennsylvania, referred to the area as Ihepetonga.

Then this and that happened, George Washington and the Revolution, Fort Defiance, British occupation, all kinds of people were born and they lived and died and then in the 1840s they began to build ports to serve as the offloading end of the Erie Canal.

From the time the Atlantic Basin was dredged and opened around 1850, right up until technology changed everything over 100 years later, Red Hook's ports were some of the busiest in the country.

H.P. Lovecraft lived in Red Hook and wrote a horror story about it. Hubert Selby Jr. lived close to Red Hook and wrote *Last Exit to Brooklyn*, published in 1964, about the dockworkers and seamy underbelly of Brooklyn's waterfront.

Arthur Miller's *A View from the Bridge* deals with the corruption of the docks, as does *On the Waterfront*, which was set in Red Hook.

The Red Hook Houses were completed in 1939 for the growing number of dockworkers. More than 20,000 were thought to live in Red Hook at various points over the next 20 years. Today it's the largest housing project in Brooklyn.

Maybe this is where Sixto raised his family. Maybe my father grew up on these streets.

Whenever I've had occasion to go to Red Hook, usually to the IKEA for bookshelves or sofas, I've imagined my father on the ballfields with his friends in the late '40s and '50s. I've wondered if he played on Bay Street or that lot between Hicks and Henry.

Dispatch From This Thing Of Ours

Crazy Joe Gallo, famous mafioso, was born in Red Hook in 1929. Bob Dylan wrote a song about him, "king of the streets, child of clay, Joey, Joey, what made them want to come and blow you away."

This was shortly after he was shot and killed at a clam house in Little Italy.

All my life I've associated Brooklyn and New York City with the mafia. The images that flash through my head come from gangster movies and television and black-and-white photographs.

My father always seemed Italian to me and I never thought of him as Puerto Rican. My mother's mother was Philomena and there was Aunt Mella and Uncle John and Uncle Joe and Aunt Mary and cousin Anthony and my father fit right in with all of them. That was our family. That's who we saw on weekends and on most holidays and more importantly that's the culture we indulged in at home. Every Sunday my mother made a gravy, that's a tomato sauce with various meats in it, hot and sweet sausage, meatballs, and braciole.

Every holiday started with the antipasto that featured dried sausage, salami and ham capicola, which was pronounced *gabagool*, roasted red peppers, fresh mozzarella and provolone, maybe some artichoke hearts and olives, and semolina bread.

My father and I watched *The Godfather*(s) together countless times, quoted from it ceaselessly.

We ate cannoli and Napoleons and pignoli, never flan or pineapple rum cake or *arroz con leche*.

I used to wonder if he ever ran into any mob types in Red Hook as a teenager in the 1950s. Maybe he was singing doo-wop with his friends on the corner, "Oh, What a Night" by the Dells or "Sincerely" by the Moonglows. And then this wise guy comes over and says if this quartet is ever interested in making any money they should let him know.

He wouldn't have anything to do with any sort of criminal behavior and as a Puerto Rican he could never become an official member.

Me, I always harbored fantasies of becoming either a mafioso or grifter and at least I was half Italian, but like Henry Hill I could never get made.

Dispatch From W.T. Clarke High School

One high school friend, George Rosado, signed my yearbook with an endearing signature, Your spic in crime, which was probably the last time I heard or read a friend refer to himself this way.

I'm sure teenagers still do this sort of thing.

Dispatch From As Certain As Longitude And Latitude

Puerto Nowhere is surrounded by the Atlantic Ocean and extends as far north as Canada and south to Chile. The eastern and western borders are boundless.

Puerto Nowhere is positioned squarely in dense urban areas and the almost as dense suburbs but rarely in any rural territories.

Puerto Nowhere enjoys a climate that is both tropical and arctic.

Dispatch From I Wish I Was In Dixie

Where I grew up, the parents dressed their children in bulky snowsuits with galoshes and ski hats, which probably bears a strong resemblance to other culturally desolate and homogenous parts of the country.

I'm talking about strip malls and fast-food chains and multiplex theaters playing all the same idiotic superhero movies. I'm talking about grown men playing video games and wearing ball caps and sneakers and driving oversized tanks and hoarding bottled water and toilet paper whenever there is a hurricane warning or global pandemic. How far too many are racist and small-minded and success is solely measured by good grades when you're in school and how much money you make after school.

I always forget how much this suburban reality bothers me until I drive past such architectural atrocities on my way to some gig or job or task. Then it all comes rushing back and I want to call in an air strike. I say out loud to my girlfriend, Jenny, that it's time to drop the big one. I've said this to her on Long Island, in Jersey, in California, in a host of other locations, including Brooklyn and Manhattan because they're both unweeded gardens grown to seed.

I don't know if parents still dress up their kids in these outfits, as I try not to look at children if I can help it.

But I was out for a walk one evening in Syracuse, New York, where I was teaching a graduate class on fragmented novels as the visiting writer for the semester. A gaggle of undergrads were up ahead of me, all clad in skin-tight black jeans with black halters exposing their midriffs and black high-heeled shoes or boots. There were about 20 of them marching through the streets in no discernible formation. At first I thought it was a dance troupe and they were on their way to a performance. But when I mentioned this to a colleague I was informed that this was a group of students on their way out to a club. She said they always look like that.

I'm certain that a good many of those students were from places exactly like Long Island.

Some places exactly like Long Island include Park Slope in Brooklyn and the Upper East Side of Manhattan, but at least in those neighborhoods you're spared the strip malls and fast-food restaurants and on occasion can see a sprinkling of freaks and weirdos who always appear lost and in need of directions.

I lived in Park Slope for a long year and a half and it was intolerable. The people were like most Long Islanders I've come across, cold and unfriendly. Mostly white, mostly rich.

My experiences living in Fort Greene and Clinton Hill from 2008 to 2020 were quite different. There was often a sense of community walking those streets. People smiling at each other and saying hello.

I'm not sure it's the same anymore. Maybe it's due to Covid, maybe it's a new breed of gentrifiers.

I didn't come close to seeing or feeling this sense of community in Park Slope and I can't recall anyone smiling or saying hello to me even once.

Brooklyn is unrecognizable today from even 15 years ago. The ever-growing population of high-rises downtown defile the once open skyline and the traffic is thick with aggressive and unruly drivers. Everywhere you look there's an absurd store dedicated to boutique mayonnaise or overpriced throw rugs and pouffes and there's indoor rock climbing and lots of money and honking car horns.

The world is not my home I'm just a-passing through, said Tom Waits.

Dispatch From Another Time, Another Place

For about 15 years I stayed away from where I did the bulk of my growing up, Long Island, central Nassau County in the town of Hempstead, where it is awful all the time. But recently I've had no choice because I took a job out on Long Island and my girlfriend's cousin lives in Port Washington.

Every time I find myself on these old stomping grounds I die a little inside.

Our parents moved us out of Brooklyn in 1973 because we all would've been killed otherwise.

Most people in New York in the 1970s were killed or mugged or raped and if you wanted your kids to grow up at all you had to move them out to the white suburbs. There they could go to school and eat fast food and play Little League baseball and shop at the mall with all the white kids already there and the other refugee children from New York City.

I remember my father and cousin and uncle talking about how us kids growing up on Long Island were soft and would get eaten alive if we were to even visit the city, let alone live there.

The city might as well have been a peninsula on the moon for as much connection as we had to it while growing up.

We visited our relatives in the boroughs, but there was no other reason to go into the city.

So much has disappeared for me in this country, these so-called United States of America, *where I was born, early Lord one frosty morn*, including language and culture and memory.

Disappeared before I knew it was ever there in the first place, long before I was born into these circumstances, which is a particular kind of American tragedy.

Dispatch From Hang On A Minute

Which isn't to say that I had an unhappy childhood at all. Everything was always fine growing up and all I cared about was sports and music and my family and that's how I filled my life.

These dyspeptic feelings for Long Island were only acquired in retrospect. They've been grandfathered in. I didn't realize how small-minded and colorless and culturally bankrupt everyone was until I left.

I'm not sure this is entirely true.

The truth is I did realize it at the time, but it took me a while to escape.

Dispatch From A Slice Of Paradise

In early 2022 *The New York Times* reported that many rich Americans were buying property in Puerto Rico due to significant tax incentives and that people can work from home and home can be anywhere.

Puerto Rico has been in dire financial straits for years and the influx of wealthy investors might help some Puerto Ricans, but others are being forced out of their homes because they can no longer afford them.

A resident of Rincón said, It feels like Hurricane Maria placed a "For Sale" sign on the island.

According to the article, 43% of Puerto Ricans live under the federal poverty level.

Dispatch From Gates Between Franklin And Classon

Now I live on the border of Clinton Hill and Bedford-Stuyvesant in Brooklyn. There's a Baptist church directly across the street from our apartment. Close by there's a mosque and a synagogue and all kinds of taco joints and a Korean barbeque and an Ethiopian place which is on the same street as a Nigerian restaurant and three Italian trattorias.

Walk around these neighborhoods in Brooklyn and you see everybody from everywhere, and you hear French and Spanish and Korean and accents from the Caribbean and Africa and you see scaffolding and cranes and kids on scooters and delivery men on motorized bikes and farmers' markets and artisanal vegan ice cream shops and you smell pot smoke. You can't go two blocks without smelling the skunk.

This is life in Brooklyn now.

Years ago my mother said that my father would get a kick out of me living in Brooklyn. I know that's true and there's a part of me that feels like I've come home for the both of us, but then there's another part that feels like I was abducted and held hostage for a long time and by the time I returned home was unrecognizable.

Dispatch From The Mistakes Both God And I Make

Church was always recognizable and predictable, but we hardly ever went to church when I was growing up.

I'd had all of the prayers and rituals and benedictions memorized even though we rarely attended mass except on the occasional Easter or Christmas Eve. The sitting, the standing and kneeling, the peace be unto you and also with you.

I was always good at memorizing language, songs and prayers and poems.

No one I knew went to church very often or was religious in any tangible way. This was my little corner of the Long Island of the 1970s and '80s, which led me to conclude the whole country had gone secular, that if God wasn't necessarily dead he was on indefinite hiatus.

Almost the same way so many concluded that we lived in a post-racial society after the election of our first Black president.

Who, like me and a growing number of countless others, is half one thing and half another.

Dispatch From The City Of Pure Waters

I always thought it peculiar that the Puerto Rican side of my family was nonexistent, but I never cared. I didn't hear much about the Italian side of my family, either, at least as far as history goes. I heard a slew of names attached to aunts, uncles, and cousins, Nicolinas, Johnnyboys, Ralphies, and I saw most of them at holidays and that was enough. But there was never a narrative attached to an ancestor like you see in the movies. My great-great-so-and-so came to this country with nothing but the shirt on his back and 24 cents in his pocket.

I didn't realize that I was missing an essential part of who I am, that is, where I come from. For most of my time on this planet I've had other things to think about and a life to make but here I am approaching 50 and this hole feels like as much a part of who I am as anything else.

Assimilation is one thing, but eradicating history and culture and language is another, which is what's happened to me and who knows how many others.

Perhaps this is the fallout of assimilation, the disconnection that is everywhere in my life as an ersatz Latino. In a lot of ways I'm a LINO as a result, Latino in name only.

It doesn't seem quite like collateral damage, but maybe that's a good analogy.

The words that come to mind are destructive, the end result of a bombing—annihilation, obliteration, casualties.

Dispatch From The Pool Of Bethesda

I remember hearing the name of a church or school all through my teenage years. Apparently a number of my friends were confirmed there or played football in the field behind the building. They called it Saint Rayfields. I didn't know where it was and had never seen it.

I did this quite a lot as a teenager, play along as if I knew what everyone was talking about instead of asking questions.

Around this time I was in the market for a used car, as were any number of my classmates and teammates. It was a rite of passage on Long Island, as nothing was within walking distance and no one walked anywhere.

I needed a car to drive back and forth to school and practice and the part-time job at my friend John's father's delicatessen, where I pretended I knew how to work the slicer and hoped I didn't amputate a finger.

I'd first wanted Kenny Ono's red 1985 Trans-Am that he was trying to unload for 1,500 dollars. The car was immaculate and in good condition from every angle, inside and out. It had no scratches or dents and the interior was pristine and the mileage wasn't prohibitive.

I'd arranged for Kenny to bring it over to my house one day for my father to test-drive, as he would either give me the green light or tell me to forget it.

Kenny and I waited on the street while my dad drove off and around the block, out of sight. He was gone for a few minutes and returned with some jive about the transmission slipping.

Months later I was dragooned into buying a 1977 Oldsmobile Delta 88, which was the size of a city bus, for 1,800 dollars. Every part of this car resembled a decommissioned tank from WWII, except for the color, banana yellow.

I was going to be safe in this car; presumably due to its size and that it refused to go faster than 60 miles per hour.

I drove this jalopy for a year before it gave out. I never went anywhere exciting, as I didn't think I should drive it for more than 20 minutes at a time. The car would make unholy sounds and start to shake like an epileptic in the throes of a seizure. It was a yearlong death rattle.

Once I drove past a church no more than ten minutes from my house. The sign out front said—San Raphael's.

I think it took me weeks or months or years to put two and two together.

This is what they were referring to; this was the church.

Saint Rayfields.

A whiteout is when there's a blizzard that reduces visibility to near zero.

Dispatch From The Kamby Bolongo

I think about Alex Haley and how he was able to trace his family's history back 200 years to a teenager in Africa named Kunta Kinte. How he did this through an oral tradition that was passed down from The Gambia to Virginia, from the 18th century to the 20th, and how there was never a break in that chain despite the unspeakable horrors of slavery.

Of course, the differences are extraordinarily profound—immigrating in hopes of a better life, and getting captured for the purpose of being the legal property of a white man.

For Kunta Kinte the practice of passing along language and culture to his daughter, Kizzy, who passed it along to her son, George, who passed it down to his sons and so forth, was a defiant act, one of courage, desperation, and an abundant pride in who he was and where he came from.

For Sixto Lopez the practice of not passing along language and culture to his son, Robert, who therefore couldn't pass it along to his son Robert, was probably done out of a perceived necessity and perhaps desperation, as well. This is what you have to do to make it here as an American so to hell with pride.

The end result is my father never spoke Spanish but he did have high blood pressure and headaches from high blood pressure, and my mother is Italian but doesn't speak Italian and had the TIA and a whole day lost to the amnesia business.

This is what I've inherited, the potential for something to go wrong with the two most important organs in my body, though so far I've been lucky. But I'm always waiting for the day to come, when the pounding in my temples finally sends me to the hospital.

It's funny what is passed on and what isn't, what's inherited and what disappears.

I can't count how many times someone has spoken Spanish to me and I've had to say, I'm sorry, I don't speak Spanish.

No hablo español, lo siento.

Dispatch From The Mango City

Once I asked a line cook named Visita, who was called Busy for short, what *pendejo* meant. This was a time before the Internet and thus one had to rely on people or visit a library to acquire information. He said it meant goddammit, which isn't true. I wasn't sure if he didn't know the English word himself or didn't want me to know it, wanted me to remain ignorant.

Most of the time I took the ribbing as good-natured because I'm sure it was. As I got to know all of them better, Jose and Roy and Chino and Fausto, they became my friends, in a manner of speaking, which is to say, not at all. I was cordial with them and joked around with them, but we never hung out outside of work or talked about what was going on in our lives, what was right or wrong. I'd bring them a beer, ask them to make dinner for me, cook something myself for them. I'd like to think I asked about their kids but if I did I doubt I actually cared about the answers. We were civil and collegial like countless other workplace relationships that don't venture beyond the workplace.

But perhaps there was some resentment on their part that I was in the front of the house, making better money like the rest of the gringos while there they were sweating it out in the back, slaving over deep fryers and hot ovens for light paychecks.

I'm not sure that learning Spanish now would fix any of this, would fix anything at all.

Dispatch From Court 4, Fort Greene Park

1,500 miles from Puerto Rico, I have a friend who, every time she sees me, asks if I've lost weight and the answer is maybe one day or wouldn't that be nice or I don't see it happening. I can tell her I don't own a scale so I can't say one way or the other. I can tell her that my grandfather lost weight but only when he was sick and dying from cancer and that my father never lost weight and never even tried.

So many miles from Puerto Rico, I tell my friend that when I meet students for the first time in a class setting, I go around the room and ask what they had for breakfast. Someone might say oatmeal and I'll ask if it was steel-cut or instant. Then I'll ask what they put in the oatmeal and if the answer doesn't include fruit or berries and maple syrup or honey and either almond, walnut, or pecan, then I will admonish them. Once someone said they had a tuna sandwich and there was a bell pepper in it and I asked them to leave the room.

I have no idea what my grandfather ate for breakfast in Puerto Rico or in Brooklyn. I don't tell my friend that I'm not sure what my father would have for breakfast every day because he was up and out of the house before the rest of us, but he brought home bacon, egg, and cheese sandwiches from the deli on the weekends and we would eat at the kitchen table while reading the papers.

Dispatch From You Better Get Organized Quick

When it comes to being Latino or Puerto Rican, I only know what I've read in books or seen in movies.

That's the kind of Latino I am, how I was made.

Families are always rising and falling in America, said a character in *The Departed*, who claimed that Nathaniel Hawthorne said it first.

We can amend this one to dying and disappearing, too.

Dispatch From Starrett City

We'd drive out on holidays, birthdays, and the occasional Sunday to visit my grandparents in Starrett City, Brooklyn. My sister and I would sit in the back seat while we drove the length of the Southern State Parkway, which turned into the Belt once you hit Queens, which you usually did with great trepidation, as the traffic was always murderous. That's what people would say, they'd say the traffic was murder.

The memories I have of my grandfather are fractured and fragmented. Him pronouncing *pumpkin pie* in an exaggerated manner, puffing out his cheeks like Dizzy Gillespie at the beginning of each word. We'd visit them every Thanksgiving and this was his opportunity for doing this. After the final chorus of the insipid Happy Birthday song, he would add an ominous and hilarious coda: …How many more? There was a standup keyboard in their apartment and I remember him playing *The Godfather* theme, "Speak Softly Love." He also owned a guitar, but I have no memory of him playing guitar. He was a good cook, but I only remember him cooking pork chops with rice and beans—*arroz con chuletas*, although he didn't call it that—or a turkey on Thanksgiving. His secret was laying strips of bacon on top of the turkey as it cooked.

Starrett City is a housing complex that opened in 1974 on a peninsula on the north shore of Jamaica Bay. It is located in the Spring Creek section of East New York.

From the beginning Starrett City housed individuals on the basis of an affirmative action program wherein 70% of households went to non-Hispanic white families and the other 30% to minority families. In 1976, those minority households were 19% Black, 9% Hispanic, and 2% Asian. (I imagine my grandparents were part of the 9%.) By 1979 the proportion of white residents declined to 64%. At the time advertisements for Starrett City featured testimonials from mostly white residents, but applicants were far more often non-white than white. Due to the racial quotas, Black applicants waited for apartments in Starrett City nearly eight times as long as white applicants. By 1983 the development's 5,881 apartments were fully occupied and of the 6,000 families on its waiting list, 75% were minorities.

As a musician you have to keep one foot back in the past and have one foot forward into the future, Dizzy Gillespie is quoted as saying.

In 1979 a group of Black families represented by the National Association for the Advancement of Colored People initiated a class-action suit against Starrett City and the maintenance of its quota system. In May 1984 it was settled that Starrett City would increase the number of apartments for minorities by 175, and the ratio of non-Hispanic white to minority families soon changed from 65% to 35%.

Of course, I didn't know anything about this when we would visit my grandparents on weekends and holidays. The people I saw walking the halls of their building or the streets surrounding it were as old as my grandparents so I thought it was a community for retired persons who were waiting to die any minute.

Rather than an old folks' home it was an old folks' city, like what went on in Florida.

The people I saw were city people to my eyes, meaning they were white and Black and brown. Though perhaps too many were white as mandated by the quota.

Give us your tired, your poor, but no more than 30%.

Dispatch From 21 Hark Lane

Spic and Span is a cleaning product I remember from childhood. It was always advertised on television but I haven't seen one of their commercials since the '70s or '80s.

Minnie Pearl said it helps your floor show its true colors.

Maybe it's not around anymore.

Dispatch From Madrid Or Valencia
Or Barcelona Or Wherever

I tend to understand the Spanish spoken by Spaniards a lot easier than those from Latin America. To my ear, Spaniards enunciate and I can discern where one word or sentence ends and the next begins.

Most Latin Americans I've heard speak ten miles a minute and I often try and fail to pick out familiar sounds in their machine-gun delivery.

I mentioned this to my friend Kenny once and he said that for him it was the other way around with Spaniards and Latin Americans.

But he's half Italian, half Jewish and his serve is only tricky because he's left-handed.

I used to read Neruda poems with an ex-girlfriend and it didn't sound half bad. I can pronounce many words properly.

I can roll Rs with the best of them.

Dispatch From Havana

I'd butcher a lot of words, too, particularly multisyllabic jobs like *temerariamente* or *adormecida*.

As I type this I have tennis on in the background, picture, no sound. Women's doubles at the Australian Open. Brady/Riske vs. Chan/Chan.

My father would shout *uzule* whenever the sun would finally emerge on a gloomy day. I always assumed it was Spanish, but it was just a word he made up.

Perhaps he got *uzule* from *luz del sol* which means sunlight. Perhaps it was a creative dyslexic bastardization.

We'd be in the living room, which had a floor-to-ceiling window, and maybe I had a baseball game that night and it was looking doubtful and then the entire room would get flooded with light and my father would shout *uzule* and that meant maybe the game wouldn't get rained out.

I'm trying to recall other such neologisms but the only one I can think of might be spelled *shallabullatay* and was pronounced like *shambala*. This word didn't seem attached to any sort of definition.

My father loved the sun and warm weather and I have always been the opposite.

He had dreams of retiring to Florida and buying a boat.

I only go to Florida if someone is paying me and I prefer dry land.

I play my best tennis in the fall and winter and always like it when the sun decides to stay home instead of baking and blinding me on the court.

"Chan Chan" is a song written by Compay Segundo and performed by the Buena Vista Social Club.

The window in our living room wasn't exactly floor to ceiling, but it was large enough and I remember sitting inside with the air conditioning, looking out at my father sitting outside on the deck.

"Chan Chan" and "Guantanamera" are two songs I can sing in very passable Spanish, though I won't know what most of the lyrics mean.

Dispatch From Meadowbrook Elementary

Vinny called me a spic one day in the fifth or sixth grade and this meant I had to fight him. I can't remember if we fought during recess or after school, but it couldn't have been in winter after a snowstorm. You couldn't have a proper fight while dressed in one of those snowsuits and Vinny and I had a proper fight, one that involved jabs and uppercuts and wrestling moves and tight clinches.

Vinny was Italian and a year older because he'd been left behind and at that age one year makes a difference. He was the biggest and strongest kid in the school but I was fearless and probably stupid back then and I fought him in the playground to a respectable draw.

It was quick and fast and involved a mixture of wrestling and boxing and square dancing. I was probably jacked up on adrenaline because this was the first time I'd ever fought anyone who was outside my own weight class.

Someone broke up the fight, probably a teacher, because kids always like to watch other kids fight each other.

But it's possible we stopped fighting on our own when we realized neither was going to win nor quit.

Back then I'd get very angry whenever someone called me a spic. I didn't know what it meant but I knew it had something to do with my Latin heritage and I knew it wasn't a compliment.

Now I couldn't care less were someone to call me a spic, though no one has, not for 30 years.

I'm sure it's because I live in Brooklyn and am surrounded by the liberal rainbow of ethnicities and cultures exemplified by my tennis community.

Had I been living in the South or Midwest someone might have called me a spic sometime in the last 30 years, maybe.

Seems more likely to have it happen recently.

We're living in a golden age for racists.

Dispatch From Borinquen

Sixto busking on a street corner in Mayagüez. He has a straw hat to collect coins and notes, but it's 1918 so no one tips a street musician with notes. He knows only four songs including "Guantanamera," which, even though it's a Cuban song and wouldn't be written for another ten years, Sixto plays anyway.

Everyone passing by takes notice of him, but few stop to listen and even fewer drop money into the straw hat. He's hoping to make enough for a lunch of *empanadillas* at the *cantina* down the street. Last week he could only afford one, but an ancient old man named Hector told him if he took his time and savored each bite he could make the meat-filled pastry last for an hour and then one *empanadilla* could keep him satisfied until dinner.

Dispatch From The Back Of A Paddy Wagon

I did get into a few fights as a kid, but only a few. All the fights were one on one and quick and fast and idiotic like the one with Vinny. They never involved weapons, no guns or knives or baseball bats.

It wasn't like in *West Side Story* with the rumbles between the Puerto Ricans and white kids and racist cops rousting and harassing everyone.

I can't remember if the Puerto Ricans were the Sharks or the Jets, but I do remember thinking the whole thing was ridiculous.

We were told if there was ever real trouble, if you needed help, you called the police. The police were nice men who would help if you were lost, if your car broke down, if some older kids were about to start trouble.

I can't remember exactly when I started being skeptical of the police. Maybe it was after Rodney King got the hell beat out of him by an army of brutal cops in California.

My parents didn't have to give me the talk that all Black kids received about the police. Not as a half Puerto Rican growing up on Long Island in the 1970s and '80s.

I'd be in a delicatessen, waiting on a sandwich, and two cops would be in front of me. I started to wonder, Why do these people need guns strapped to their hips? What would happen if I ripped one out of its holster?

The village I grew up in, Westbury, was entirely white south of Jericho Turnpike and mostly Black north of it with a few real Latinas mixed in, ones who spoke Spanish and whose skin was a little darker than mine.

I'd like to say that once we came of age we'd drive over to the poor side of town where we'd chase after girls named Anita and Esperanza. That we couldn't resist their dark eyes and hair and their shapely hips and the way they dressed and their fiery temperaments. We'd take them to dances and movies and their older brothers would chase after us with switchblades and billy clubs.

But, of course, none of this happened.

The Black and Latino kids attended Westbury High School, the white kids W.T. Clarke and never the twain did meet except on basketball courts and baseball diamonds.

Nothing dramatic ever happened, nothing that would make the news.

Except once when a kid named Carter got himself killed in a backyard fight at a house party. Someone slashed his neck or shoulder and he bled out in front of everyone. I don't know who killed him or if they called the police or if anyone was ever arrested. My friend Mike had mentioned something about that party earlier in the day, but I hadn't felt like going.

Dispatch From The Open Field
Outside My Childhood Home

One vaporous memory ... my father and grandfather and me on the baseball field outside of my house. I'm maybe seven or eight or ten years old and I'm hitting fungoes to them. A fungo is traditionally hit with a fungo bat, which is much lighter and thinner than a regulation bat and thus enables one to easily loft the ball into the air. Baseball coaches do this every day when it comes time for the outfielders to shag flies. My father was great at this and I became quite adept at catching sky-high pop-ups by the age of five. By the time I was a teenager I could catch the ball behind my back, which you'd never do in a game, of course. But after fielding thousands of these over the years, players become bored and have to do tricks to keep both engaged and amused.

On this day I wanted to hit, as I was always out in the field with a glove on my hand. And I probably wanted to show my grandfather that I could hit as well as I could field. But I couldn't get the ball in the air on any of my two thousand attempts.

I can still see my grandfather trotting after a ball I scorched at him on the ground, a hot shot instead of a can of corn.

I felt bad about this. He would've been in his mid-70s and a man that old shouldn't ever have to bend over to field a ground ball.

My father rightly admonished me and I had to hand the bat back over to him.

No man over 45 should ever have to field a ground ball, said Diego Goldstein.

I remember my grandfather's fingernails, how there was a fold down the middle, as if they'd been bent inward. I think my father's fingernails caved in the same way toward the end of his life. As of today, this hasn't happened to me.

My grandfather was probably five foot five or six, several inches shorter than my father. This led my father to believe that I'd continue the trend and shoot up past him. My whole life I heard him say about me, he's going to be a six-footer.

I almost made it; fell short by only four or five inches.

Dispatch From Pennsylvania Avenue

My sister remembers our grandfather pretending to kill bugs on our heads. He'd squeeze those bent fingernails together and make a clicking sound on our scalps. She remembers him making *plátanos*, which I don't at all remember. I do remember rice and beans and pork chops, but that was the only Spanish culture or cuisine I was exposed to growing up. We had it at my grandparents', but never at home.

My sister remembers their apartment on Pennsylvania Avenue in Starrett City, 4-H, and the aroma of our grandfather's cooking when she went through the door.

I loved to watch my grandfather eat. It's as if he made love to the food, gently caressing the grains of rice back and forth before inviting them up and onto his fork. To this day I've never seen anyone eat like him, nor have I seen anyone take as long to finish a meal. The rest of the family would leave him at the table to go off into the living room and he would sit by himself for another 15 or 20 minutes.

Of course, now I wish I'd stayed behind. Asked him questions about Puerto Rico and his life there, when and why he immigrated to Brooklyn, where and how he met my grandmother, if anyone had ever called him a spic or how often, what he did for a living, what he wanted for his children, what he wanted for me, my sister. I can think of a million questions now.

I might've been able to save my family had I done this.

Dispatch From All Of It

My mother still can't remember what happened that morning she lost to the amnesia, but she can remember the day before and the day after. She can go backward or forward and pretend like nothing happened, because in a way nothing did.

But I can't go back 75 years to fix my problem, to make an argument for maintaining our family's history, our language, thus gaining a foothold into what it means to be Puerto Rican, what it means to be this particular Lopez line of Puerto Ricans.

And all the while I'm thinking, I play tennis with a Chinese man who speaks Spanish and I am a Puerto Rican who doesn't.

I can't decide if this is absurd or beautiful or tragic. Probably it's all of it.

Dispatch From Center Court

I sometimes wonder how much better I'd be if I'd started playing when I was a kid. That instead of a baseball bat I wielded a racket.

Everyone comments on my unorthodox slice forehand, which is tough to deal with, as hardly anyone employs the maneuver, which is essentially a squash shot. There is not much margin as the ball crosses the net and stays very low to the court due to the underspin. The shot has a lot of pace on it and my opponents and hitting partners have to move in and bend down to get it back.

This shot comes from my background and training as a baseball player. Years ago players were encouraged to have a level swing, even swinging down on the ball to hit hard line drives. This is the antithesis of how tennis players are trained to hit the ball, which is always from low to high, turning the wrist over to apply topspin to the ball.

I do hit the ball "properly," from low to high, when the strike point is anywhere from my waist down to my shoe tops. But it's clear I'm self-taught, though hitting a moving ball with a stick has always come naturally and feels great when you do so on the screws, which is a baseball term.

That I get to play with former college players is something I enjoy and take a certain measure of pride in. In fact, I sometimes hit with a guy who was ranked as a junior, played in college, and once beat a guy who played in the US Open. He also once beat a guy, who beat a guy, who beat Nadal.

So when I aced him twice during a tiebreak it was tantamount to acing Nadal.

Tennis is the only arena wherein I accept and promote this sort of six degrees of separation idiocy.

Although, I'm not sure I'd accept or promote it on anyone else's behalf.

Granted, this friend I hit with, named Jackson, is two levels better than me, at least, maybe three. I sometimes start laughing when he opens up on a forehand and I hear it sizzling by me. I can actually hear the ball rotating violently through the air. Still, I can hang with Jackson a little, give him something of a workout, take a few points off him, but if it ever came to push and shove I'd have no chance.

Nadal reminds me of the marauding Spaniards, the ones who traversed the ocean blue to find gold and slaves and land and women. He treats his opponents mercilessly, like a colonist.

Dispatch From The Mountaintop

I've never been ashamed or embarrassed that I don't speak Spanish. It has nothing to do with me; I wasn't responsible, like the color of my skin or my height, which is five-eight when I take my vitamins.

What I do feel is an ambivalence I can't quite wrap my head around.

After all, the assimilation was successful. Sixto Lopez's grandson went to college, obtained an advanced degree, authored books, and became a college professor. His granddaughter also has a master's degree and lives a thoroughly assimilated and comfortable life in suburban New Jersey surrounded by white people.

I was the first person on either side of my family to attend a college or university, let alone graduate. This could've been quite the victory for certain members of my family, but there weren't any celebrations. Almost everyone from my public high school on Long Island went to college. In my little white world it was routine. And I didn't put any effort into high school and that nonexistent work ethic continued as an undergraduate so none of it seemed like an accomplishment to me.

My father encouraged me to take a civil service exam so I could have something to fall back on. By then I'd graduated with a degree in communications and was working in restaurants part-time while reading and writing full-time. All with designs on the life that I would eventually lead as a writer and educator. Such pursuits would've been entirely unthinkable to my grandfather. Even my father, who lived long enough to see me get into graduate school, couldn't quite imagine it.

There were no bookcases in my grandparents' apartment.

We had some built-in bookshelves in our den and there was a set of junior encyclopedias but I don't remember any other books. My mother read bestsellers and mysteries but she was the only reader I knew and I had no interest in books beyond biographies of Elvis or Wayne Gretzky until I turned 22.

My father, after serving in the army, worked a host of jobs as a single man and was employed by IBM and UPS, amongst others. He once studied to be a court reporter. He wanted to take courses in horticulture at SUNY Farmingdale and applied under the GI Bill, but didn't pursue it. Once he married and started a family he landed a job with the New York City Department of Sanitation and became a garbage man. He did this for 22 years before retiring.

The thinking was he did all of this for my sister and me so that we could do better. So that we wouldn't have to really work for a living, wouldn't have to muscle our way through life.

Assimilation is a long-range plan that takes foresight, patience, and sacrifice.

All of which reminds me of Martin Luther King Jr.'s mountaintop speech: "I've been to the mountaintop ... I've seen the Promised Land. I may not get there with you. But I want you to know tonight, that we, as a people, will get to the Promised Land."

It's the sacrifice I find most compelling. I see my father as having sacrificed to a certain degree to provide for his family. Getting up at a god-awful hour of the morning, working outside in the scorching heat and freezing cold, working the body to the point of exhaustion.

This is something I try to keep in mind, live up to and earn, but it's not like I feel pressure about it. I do a good job of putting all of that out of my head.

Dispatch From The Points That Matter

In this way I'm like the best tennis players, who always seem impervious to pressure. The best players win the big points, the points that matter. Roger Federer, arguably the greatest player of all time, *only* wins around 55% of the total points he plays. The difference is when it comes time to step up he's able to raise his level. One imagines the great players reaching a higher plane of existence where the mind is emptied and the focus is only on the here and now, see the ball and hit it.

I can only do this sporadically on the court. Too often I'll tighten up and make the unforced error that has me cursing myself and questioning why the hell I play this game.

I appreciate what my father did for me and what his father did for both of us. But sacrificing our language and culture, our heritage and history, didn't have to be part of the bargain.

Assimilation and erasure—a case study.

Dispatch From The Saber And Gun

Cavemen would walk back into the village after a hunt with their kill on full display. It's easy to imagine them walking slowly, playing to the crowd of appreciative and adoring onlookers.

We believe this happened due to depictions of such scenes in cave art, which was a primitive form of Instagram.

A parade is a moving village.

I like being part of a team and have missed it since I quit playing baseball. I like being in cahoots, part of a conspiracy. This is one of the great draws of my tennis community. I can go to the park pretty much anytime and run into at least a few people I know and can count as friends. It's the only arena in my life where such is the case.

I've never been a regular at any bars and I've never joined any sort of club and I've never felt like I was part of a faculty in the 20 years I taught at The New School or the 15 I taught at Pratt Institute.

I've always been an independent contractor, an underpaid mercenary, in the academic world.

I'm not a member of a political party and am registered as an independent.

I don't care for large gatherings under any circumstances, particularly where nothing is actually happening, no event is really taking place, no one is singing or dancing or playing to an audience that can enjoy the performance.

I don't like the idea of marching.

I also don't like watching Nadal play tennis. It's not his game, of course, which is a combination of extraordinary strength and will, not to mention talent. He is muscular and thick and plays the game like an onrushing bull, which is admirable. More than any other player currently on tour he seems entirely indefatigable and sometimes superhuman. He has had more than his share of injuries and has missed months of each season for years now, but this seems inevitable given the reckless abandon he exhibits on the court in every single match and with every single ball.

I learned something about Nadal recently that also impressed me, that he's naturally right-handed. There's no doubt that both tennis and baseball favor left-handers and I assume his longtime coach, his Uncle Toni, put the racket in his left hand from the time little Rafa could fully grip one.

My grandfather tried to do the same thing with my sister but in reverse, turn a natural lefty into a righty. But his motive was guided by superstition, not athletic glory.

The reason I don't like watching Nadal has nothing to do with tennis, but rather it's his oft-discussed idiosyncrasies I find off-putting. The man is obsessive compulsive to the nth degree and goes through a series of unfortunate routines while playing.

It is entirely undignified, this fount of quirks and rituals. Some of which seem superstitious and innocuous. Ultimately who cares how he drinks from what bottle or where he places the bottles on whichever lines facing whatever direction each and every time he takes a slug. But it's when he fiddles with his hair and shirt and nose in a sequential progression that looks like he's crossing himself before each serve, which then culminates with reaching into the chasm of his posterior to pick at his shorts, that I lose my mind.

I Ain't Marching Any More, said Phil Ochs.

Sixto in the living room of his son's house on Long Island and on the carpet below him his two-year-old granddaughter, Christine, all sprawled out and playing with dolls and coloring books. He sees her pick up the crayons with her left hand and beckons her to him. He tells her she isn't doing it correctly, that she needs to use her right hand. He tells her that left-handers are wicked and evil.

Nadal continues his routines when he receives a serve, as well, touching too many parts of himself. Which means he does this hundreds of times per match.

It's exhausting.

Dispatch From Puerto Nowhere

One winter I found that I was unable to leave the house. Otherwise, I was unwilling to leave the house. Either way, I didn't leave the house.

This was before Covid, maybe by three or four years.

It's not as if I was afraid of the cold or dark. I couldn't be bothered.

It lasted till spring.

Dispatch From Franklin Park

I talk to my mother on the telephone every day and once I mentioned that I was going to Crown Heights to attend a reading and she asked if it was safe.

She asked a man named Robert Lopez, he of the shaved head and salt-and-pepper beard, aged anywhere from mid-30s to mid-40s, though while only five feet eight inches tall, weighs in at a robust and muscular 190 pounds. Every part of him is muscular, save the abdominal region.

In truth, I am built like a retired running back, one who has been drinking too much beer of late but whom you still wouldn't want to fuck with, based on appearances.

My vice is pasta, not beer, as I only drink maybe one beer every so often in the summer, but who cares.

But to my mother, in her mind's eye, I am still the five-year-old boy out in the backyard with his sister, building a snow fort, who is anywhere from one to six years away from being called a spic for the first time.

She probably remembered Crown Heights from the race riot in 1991 between Black residents and Orthodox Jews. If she didn't remember the event specifically, then she, like countless others, associates certain New York City neighborhoods with crime and danger. Crown Heights, Bedford-Stuyvesant, Bushwick, Harlem, Washington Heights.

I enjoyed telling her that when white people categorize a neighborhood as unsafe it's because there are people like me, olive-skinned men and men with darker skin and we all have shaved heads or afros and we're walking around, looking menacing. I'm part of what makes it unsafe.

When I told my mother that I was called a spic as a kid she had no idea.

Dispatch From Ipswich, Great Britain

V.S. Pritchett is quoted as saying of short stories that they are glimpsed from the corner of the eye, in passing. I tell this to my students all the time, every semester.

What I don't tell them is that it's true about so much else, that it's true about everything. I don't tell them anything about my family, about my grandfather and how he died when I was 16 and I didn't know him at all, and what's more, that I don't know anything about him, either, other than how he ate his meals.

I actually do tell them that it's true about everything else, but they don't believe it.

I can't get a good look at anything it seems. There's always nothing to see or what there was to see faded out of sight a while back.

Dispatch From A Fallacy Of False Memories

Sometimes I say emigrated from Puerto Rico because Puerto Rico has never been a part of the United States.

In theory, you can't emigrate from Puerto Rico to the United States since you're already part of the United States.

In theory, Sixto wasn't an immigrant, but of course he was.

I asked my sister what she remembered of our grandfather's death. She mentioned our father getting the call at home. I told her what I remembered and she said yes, I was right. That he wasn't home when he received the call and we only saw him later after he'd already been to Brooklyn and did whatever he did there. Then she mentioned him hanging his head over the burner, too, which served as corroboration for the both of us.

She said, Your own childhood is one big fallacy of false memories.

My sister said she remembers talking to our grandfather on the phone, said it was much harder to understand him than in person. She said she remembers that he had a banjo.

He didn't have a banjo. He had the guitar. I never heard him play it or I did but I don't remember.

I know that he hated Henry Fonda. I don't know why, though I can imagine why someone would hate Henry Fonda.

No one wants to see some rich guy playing poor Tom Joad's blues in every picture or a Mexican priest or some other kind of unbearably earnest do-gooder.

But he also saved that Puerto Rican kid from Lee J. Cobb and the chair in *12 Angry Men*.

Maybe Sixto hated Fonda because he saved the young Puerto Rican thug who probably killed his father.

Maybe he hated him because he represented a kind of America that had nothing to do with Sixto.

I remember him saying that if we crossed our eyes and a fly happened past they'd get stuck like that forever.

My sister and I both remember hearing stories of how he tried to turn my sister into a right-handed person when she started exhibiting left-handed tendencies.

Dispatch From A Fascinating Version Of History

November 19, 1493—Christopher Columbus, whose name was Cristoforo Colombo or Cristóbal Colón and was born in Italy or Spain or Poland or Greece, is the first European to land on Puerto Rico.

Before that the Ortoiroid people, who moved from South America into the Caribbean around 1000 BC, were the first to settle on Puerto Rico, according to some sources.

The Taíno were the dominant indigenous culture when Columbus showed up and they started getting killed off in large numbers during the 16th century due to disease and war courtesy of the Spaniards.

Ponce de León founds the first permanent Spanish settlement on Puerto Rico in 1508.

Ponce de León discovers the fountain of youth, but it's in Florida, so who cares.

Puerto Rico belongs to Spain.

The British try multiple attacks to claim Puerto Rico as their own and fail each time.

The Dutch try and fail at the same maneuver at least once.

Then in 1898 the U.S. declares war on Spain and invades Puerto Rico.

Over in Cuba, future president Theodore Roosevelt was part of the crew who charged up San Juan Hill and defeated the Spanish there.

Spain surrenders and pulls out of Cuba and Puerto Rico.

Puerto Rico becomes a part of the United States, sort of.

Dispatch From The World As Imposition

One April I found myself on a plane to Orlando, Florida, as I was scheduled to read at the University of Central Florida. They were paying me to do this, otherwise, I'd never. No one would probably.

My girlfriend and I woke early and she drove me to Manhattan Island, which I try hard to avoid, so I could catch a car to the airport in Newark from there. We figured this would cut the cost in half, which it did. It's usually a surprise when something goes according to plan.

I hate waking early and whenever I do have to wake early I can never fall asleep the night before.

Perhaps this wouldn't qualify as herculean for most people but waking early and going into Manhattan is borderline traumatic for those of us who've arranged our lives to start no earlier than 10 a.m. and remain in Brooklyn from reveille to lights out.

I didn't want to be on that airplane. I didn't want to be in a car on the way to the airport, certainly didn't want to be on a subway. I never take the subway anymore unless I have no other choice and lately I have no other choice only once every few months. I didn't want to go anywhere that winter and early spring, not even to the café across the street, let alone someplace that required two modes of transportation and air travel to get there.

The entire world was an imposition.

But one season bled into the next and the light lingered for hours into evening and the trees and flowers were spreading their pretty poison so there was no excuse. One had to re-enter civilization and mix with people, friends especially.

One feels the call of spring, an invitation to the imposing world, every damned year.

Dispatch From Orlando, FL

The night before the paid appearance I read with friends at a bar in Orlando, Florida. No one paid me for the bar reading, but I was told that people buy books in Orlando and that we might sell a few. Because of this I brought five copies each of my most recent novel and the first story collection published almost ten years earlier. The books weighed down my overnight bag and it was far too heavy and too much to carry, but I carried it anyway.

For years I'd scoff at what people called seasonal affective disorder, but I'd manifested at least half of the symptoms.

In truth, I didn't feel depressed every day that winter. I still periodically lost interest in activities I once enjoyed, but this seemed to be entirely capricious and unrelated to weather and light. I'm a middle-aged man and I have any number of parasomnias, so I'm often low-energy, though I do muster enough to play tennis quite a lot. I'm almost always hungry and crave pasta and bread daily, if not hourly, and perhaps I gained a few pounds that winter and I'm generally full of bitterness and rage which doesn't necessarily imply agitation, though maybe it does and I've forgotten what it is I'm talking about.

I think anyone with half a brain living in 2019 felt hopeless, but I've never felt worthless or guilty, but maybe I have felt guilt for one venial sin or another, but not for long and I don't see how that's tied to seasonal affective disorder, which I will not abbreviate to SAD under any circumstances.

I've always thought of death frequently, regardless of season.

I made the plans to visit the University of Central Florida months prior to the engagement, before winter started and I'd holed myself up to ride it out. I made the plan to visit UCF in the wake of yet another failed relationship, so there was that, too.

I needed to keep occupied, so I made plans. I thought that I'd want to go out in the world and maybe have something to look forward to and even make a little money at the same time, so I booked trips to read at colleges and universities and visit with friends who lived near those colleges and universities.

I think I knew that when the time came to actually do these things I wouldn't want to anymore.

Dispatch From Puerto Nowhere

My grandfather came to Brooklyn from Puerto Rico sometime in the 1920s. Maybe it was the '30s, but by then the Depression was on so maybe that doesn't make sense or maybe it makes the most sense.

Maybe he stopped in Saint Augustine on his way north to sample the waters of Ponce de León's fountain of youth.

But why would a young person do such a thing, so let's say he skipped Saint Augustine.

Let's say he hustled his way from Florida to Brooklyn. A series of short cons and schemes, not enough to get fat but enough to keep moving.

He ran some three-card monte, pig in a poke, and the badger game. He tried a version of the Spanish Prisoner on a Cuban businessman named Pedro, who got wise, which made Sixto have to fold the con.

I don't know what season he left the island, if it was during a brutal summer or wet winter. I don't know if he ever considered somewhere other than Brooklyn or if he did live somewhere else and didn't like it there.

But he did go out into the world and changed his life like Rilke. I don't know what prompted him to do so. I don't know if life in Puerto Rico was unbearable, if it had to do with poverty, lack of opportunity, politics. There was something of a mass exodus during this time due to a series of hurricanes wiping out the island's crops. But I was told that Sixto lived in Mayagüez, which is a small city.

Puerto Ricans first came to the U.S. in the mid to late 19th century when Puerto Rico was still under Spanish rule. Amongst the first Puerto Ricans to immigrate to New York City were political exiles against Spanish colonial rule who championed Puerto Rican independence. During most of the 19th century, Puerto Rico and Cuba were the last remaining Spanish colonies in the New World, and during the last decades of Spanish rule, the Spanish Crown would imprison or banish anyone promoting the independence of Puerto Rico or calling for liberal reforms.

Lucky that Puerto Rico became a U.S. territory in 1898 in the wake of the Spanish-American War.

I don't know if Sixto Lopez was chased out of Puerto Rico and running for his life. Maybe there was a bounty on his head, although this doesn't seem at all likely. No one in my family seemed to get into any kind of trouble.

I don't know if he had any romantic ideas as to what life might be like on the mainland. Maybe he wanted to be a musician or a silent movie star. Maybe he wanted to make his way to Hollywood and be a Puerto Rican Rudolph Valentino. I can't recall seeing any photographs of Sixto when he was young, but I suspect he was handsome, as he had a rugged yet elegant appearance as an old man. The remnants of a full head of hair, streaked gray and white as he aged, a pencil-thin mustache, and the swarthy features of a prohibition-era gangster.

Maybe he dreamed of beating Roberto Clemente to the majors by some 30 years. His son was a great athlete, excelling in most sports, and his grandson was as well. He had to have been the fountainhead of ability, but who knows. I don't know if he ever played any organized baseball either in Puerto Rico or here in the States.

When he started off for New York City I don't know what he might've looked forward to, if anything. I don't know what he was hoping to achieve or if by the time he was on that boat and shoving off he'd already regretted his decision.

More than likely he wanted to find a decent job, marry an American woman and raise a family. I don't think he ever had any ambition to run his own business or own land or accumulate great wealth because none of that came to pass.

Or maybe he tried and failed.

There are, of course, millions of immigrants who do such things and my maternal grandfather did own his own business, some sort of early recycling concern, but he was born here in New York City.

Back then there was no seasonal affective disorder, so that probably didn't play any part in Sixto's life.

Dispatch From Utica And President

The Crown Heights riots began on August 19, 1991, after a driver in the motorcade of the leader of the Chabad movement accidently struck two children of Guyanese immigrants with his car, killing one and severely injuring the other.

In its wake several Jews were seriously injured and one man was killed. A few weeks following the riot a non-Jewish man, who some believe had been mistaken for a Jew, was killed by a group of Black men.

I've been mistaken for Latino most of my life.

Once, in a restaurant while working as a waiter, I was mistaken for a terrorist.

I wore a beard back then but shaved the patch of skin under my nose and above my lip, the mustache area, like Abraham Lincoln.

One customer, an older white woman, said I looked like a terrorist.

Dispatch From Those Were The Days

Sixto hears about President Hoover's visit to Puerto Rico and knows the USS Arizona will be docked in Ponce while Hoover travels across the island. The president is scheduled to deliver a speech in San Juan to the legislature, including the Governor of Puerto Rico, Theodore Roosevelt Jr.

Sixto knows this is his chance to get off the island and so he decides to stow away on the ship. He hitches car rides to Ponce and then stakes out the Arizona for a day and a half. He watches the sailors coming and going, loading and unloading. There are men in suits who don't seem to be Navy there, too. Sixto can't seem to find a soft spot or a time to sneak aboard and realizes he'll have to find another way to the mainland.

Dispatch From More Longitude and Latitude

Puerto Nowhere is located on the water but is also landlocked.

Puerto Nowhere is a thousand miles from wherever you are but only as the crow flies.

Puerto Nowhere is the entire tri-state area from the redwood forest to the Gulf Stream waters.

Dispatch From The Ballfields Of
Bowling Green Junior High School

I was one of the very few Latinos in my neighborhood, growing up on Long Island, and it wasn't like we shared any sort of bond or formed a gang with each other.

We didn't sing and dance on rooftops, didn't call ourselves Sharks or Kings. We didn't have our own turf, which we defended with our lives.

We didn't sit together in the cafeteria; we didn't call each other *ese* or *pachuco*.

These are Mexican terms and not typically used by Puerto Ricans.

The only person who ever called me *ese* was a friend named GianCarlo, who was an Italian from West Virginia.

Although, we did share a bond, the other Latinos and I, somehow. It felt superficial at the time, but perhaps it went deeper than that. Perhaps it was intuitive, a sense that we should be bonded, that we shared certain physical features and a particular heritage and people would direct jokes about hubcaps and switchblades our way and we might make those same jokes with each other, but it was okay because none of it felt particularly real.

None of us spoke Spanish, except for the Sandoval brothers. They'd come over from somewhere in Central America and joined us in the ninth grade and seemed more Latin than the rest of us.

I remember tryouts for the ninth-grade team, which was a formality for a number of us, but they were still called tryouts. Our coach, a new one, probably had received some sort of scouting report on who was good and who wasn't, but he hadn't seen anyone play before.

So there we were that first day of tryouts and the new kid, Danny Sandoval from somewhere in godforsaken Central America, has the audacity to walk over to shortstop.

There were a few positions on the field that everyone knew you shouldn't go near, me at short, J.R. Genzale behind the plate, and Phil Schneider at first.

And Danny starts fielding ground balls and displays a cannon of an arm while throwing the ball to first. I didn't want the new coach to get too impressed with the new guy, so I started throwing the ball as hard as I could to keep up.

I never would've done this under any other circumstance, as it was the first day and it was March and cold and there was no reason to air anything out and let it fly. My position on the team was secure but you never can tell when it comes to people sometimes.

I couldn't let this spic show me up.

So I wound up hurting my arm that day and before long I had to move over to second base.

Turned out Danny wasn't that good of a baseball player, he just had that cannon for an arm. But he was a good guy and a spic like me and George, so we were friends.

I was called a spic because my last name was Lopez, maybe because my hair was dark and kinky and my eyes were brown, but no darker than anyone else's.

It never registered, didn't have anything to do with me.

But back then no one was Latin, you were Spanish, maybe Hispanic. Always spics to each other in the halls and outside on the playgrounds.

Dispatch From One Of The Great Migrations

I don't know how Sixto got himself to New York City, if he took a boat or plane or what. I don't know if he came alone or with a friend or family member. I'm pretty sure it was a boat, though, as plane travel wouldn't be a viable option for another 30 years. I don't know if the boat stopped in Florida on its way north, if Sixto disembarked and had a look around, saw that the Florida landscape with its palm trees and lush vegetation and bodies of water looked like the island where he was born and what he was running away from.

The Great Migration from Puerto Rico occurred in the decades following World War II, due to the advent of affordable plane travel and increasing availability of industrial jobs. Hundreds of thousands of Puerto Ricans migrated to New York City during this time, but my grandfather was already here, already had three children, two living long enough to see the 1950s and who were already losing their culture and heritage.

Or by then it was completely gone. There's no way of knowing, no one left to ask.

Dispatch From Up On The Roof

This is where the company is up on a rooftop and the women are pitted against the men and they sing and dance and refute each other at every turn. The women hate Puerto Rico and love New York and for the men it's the other way around.

I have no recollection of watching *West Side Story* on television as a family, but we must've at some point.

Sixto would've been 57 when it was first released, but I have no idea if he enjoyed going to the movies. I have no idea what he would've thought about Natalie Wood's Maria or that Rita Moreno was one of the few actual Puerto Ricans in the cast and how they doused her in makeup so that she'd appear darker.

Puerto Rico, my heart's devotion,
Let it sink back in the ocean,
Always the hurricanes blowing,
Always the population growing
And the money owing,
And the sunlight streaming,
And the natives steaming...
Skyscrapers bloom in America,
Cadillacs zoom in America,
Industry boom in America,
Twelve in a room in America
Lots of new housing with more space,

Lots of doors slamming in our face
I'll get a terrace apartment,
Better get rid of your accent
Life can be bright in America,
If you can fight in America
Life is all right in America,
If you're all-white in America...

The lyrics for the song "America" were written by a Jewish composer and lyricist from New York City named Stephen Sondheim.

Leonard Bernstein, also Jewish, composed the music.

There were no Puerto Rican or Latin songwriters available in 1961.

The movie was remade in 2021 with Latin actors and the same music and lyrics, with some pivotal changes to reflect the attitudes and desires of actual Puerto Ricans.

So now they don't want the island to sink back into the ocean.

Dispatch From Endless Perpetrators

When Nadal plays the always elegant Roger Federer of Switzerland it's a stark contrast of style and demeanor, as Federer is lean and graceful and glides around the court like a ballet dancer.

Federer doesn't fondle himself in front of everyone, either.

Jorge doesn't like Nadal for the same reasons, that he *picks his butt*. While we were waiting for a court we watched the semifinal on our phones, Thiem of Austria vs. Djokovic of Serbia. All of us thought neither had a chance against Nadal the next day and we were all correct.

At one point Jorge stopped watching the match to take a call from his wife. They spoke Spanish to each other, something about dinner that evening.

While Jorge is from Guatemala, I'm pretty sure his ancestors weren't natives, as he has lighter skin than I do. I suspect his people came to Guatemala from Spain, that if his people weren't the first colonists themselves, they probably hitched a ride over years later as part of subsequent waves. I can understand Jorge's Spanish better than Noë's, who is from Mexico and has darker skin and hair.

I would listen to an ex-girlfriend speaking Spanish to her Spanish friends in Barcelona and feel proud of myself for understanding maybe a quarter of what was said.

I am attracted to elegance and dignity and these days we are in short supply of both.

This speaks to my lack of connection with too many people, a fundamental lack of grace and manners. I'm turned off when someone holds a fork like it's a weapon while cutting meat, when someone invokes bathroom humor of any sort at any time, particularly during mealtime. I've always been offended by locker room talk, which by no means indicates prudishness. I can hardly stand going to a baseball or hockey game for the people around me, what they say out loud in front of everyone, how they behave in public.

The list of perpetrators is endless and most everyone is guilty of one egregious sin or another.

I know there's something wrong with me when it comes to all of this, that I'm some mixture of uptight and old-fashioned, but I'll cop to this only to a degree.

Dispatch From Panama City

The word *spic* according to most sources comes from the digging of the Panama Canal.

Writing for NPR, Juan Vidal says that in 1908 the *Saturday Evening Post* sent a reporter to Panama to write about the thousands of North American laborers digging out the canal. He kept hearing the word *spiggoty*, which he learned the northerners had taken to calling Panamanians.

As in the Panamanians saying, I don't *spiggoty* English.

My sister doesn't remember if she was ever called a spic. But I'm going to say that she probably wasn't.

I'm sure she was called other things, but none of them ethnically motivated. Her friends used to call her Coco for Coco Lopez, which is a Puerto Rican coconut product used in many popular drinks.

From there *spigotty* moved around and migrated north and morphed to *spigoties* and then shortened to *spig* and finally *spic*, where it has remained ever since.

My grandmother, Lola DeLeon, known as Delores, never tried to teach me Spanish. I don't remember her ever trying to teach my sister or me a single word.

It's possible her name was Delores and she was known as Lola.

I didn't know my grandmother's maiden name so I asked my mother, who also didn't know. She was in touch with one of my grandmother's sisters on social media and looked her up. This is when my mother told me that Grandma's last name was DeLeon.

Not five minutes after I typed DeLeon for the first time my sister said that our grandmother's last name was Colon. I asked her how she knew and she said she didn't know how she knew but was confident it was Colon.

Why she knows this and not if she was ever called a spic shouldn't call anything into question.

Colon seems right to me. It rings a faint and distant bell.

This is what happens when you come from nowhere.

I come from people who either were the people or came from the people who changed their names and only spoke English to their children and they'd forbid them from speaking Spanish or Italian, perhaps even punishing them for doing so, corporally and vigorously, so that they would grow up to be good Americans and accepted by all Americans.

Sixto spanking his eight-year-old daughter for saying, *Yo tengo hambre*, on a Thursday night at dinner time. His wife, Lola, in the bathroom, applying lipstick and eye shadow.

This was common for immigrants in this country for a long period of time, particularly the first half of the 20th century, particularly if you were working class.

It seems less common now. Yesterday on *Meet the Press*, television journalist Tom Brokaw said, I also happen to believe that the Hispanics should work harder at assimilation... They ought not to be just codified in their communities but make sure that all their kids are learning to speak English.

Dispatch From Another Time, Another Place

Here's a memory... We are all sitting in the living room of my grandparents' apartment in Starrett City except my grandmother who is doing something in the kitchen, which is separated from the living room by a wall that stops halfway into the hall. I am on the sofa with my sister and father and mother and grandfather. The television is tuned to a game of some sort. In the summer it would've been baseball. My grandfather was a Mets fan like my father and me and we pulled for Strawberry and Hernandez and Gooden and the rest of the Amazins.

Everyone is preoccupied with something. My father is reading a newspaper, likely the *Daily News* or *New York Post*. My father read three newspapers cover to cover every day, the other being *Newsday*, a fine Long Island publication. Back then the *New York Post* wasn't quite so objectionable and horrifying, as this was years before Rupert Murdoch bought the paper.

My father said that reading the Sunday *Times* was equivalent to a college education. But I didn't see a Sunday *Times* until I was in my 20s.

My mother might be reading a book; I don't know what my sister is doing. I can't describe the furniture or the walls or the décor, as I cannot recall any of it.

It is a very modest one-bedroom apartment. There might be a clock on the wall, something cheap and probably garish. There is no art on the walls, perhaps a framed picture or two of my grandmother, as she was extraordinarily vain and asked for her picture to be taken more often than anyone I've ever known.

This was well before the age of selfies, a word that makes my fingers choke as I type it out.

My grandfather very quietly whistles, a pretty note full of vibrato lasting no more than two seconds. I see his cheeks flutter.

Two seconds later my grandmother appears. She stands in the entry to the living room and listens as my grandfather asks for iced tea.

I look around to see if anyone was paying attention, if anyone caught this.

No one flinches, no one looks up. I'm the only one privy to what's happened. I was glad of this, relieved. It wouldn't have to be discussed. I wouldn't have to say the sentence out loud.

He had her trained to come when he whistled.

Of course, I was appalled, awed, dumbstruck.

This is where we say that it was a different time, a different place, a different culture. We say that Sixto Lopez was born in Mayagüez, Puerto Rico, in 1904 and we're talking about machismo and traditional gender roles and subservience. We talk about class and education, the woman's place in the kitchen and apparently at the beck and whistle of her husband.

A woman's place is right there now in her home, said Ray Charles.

Dispatch From The Golden Age

In an analysis conducted by the Pew Research Center in 2013, it was determined that more than 37 million Latinos in the U.S. spoke Spanish at home. However, while this number continues increasing because of the growth of the Latino population, the percentage of Latinos who speak the language has decreased over the years: 73% in 2015, down from 78% in 2006, according to another analysis.

In spite of this drop-off in use, in a 2011 Pew Research Center survey most Latinos agreed that speaking Spanish is essential, with nearly all surveyed responding that it is important for future generations of Latinos in the U.S. to speak Spanish. Yet another survey from 2015 found that 71% of Latinos felt it unnecessary to speak Spanish to be considered Latino.

There doesn't seem to be data from 1940 when my father was born, when they hung signs in shops that said "No Dogs or Puerto Ricans," but one imagines the numbers to be wildly different.

Dispatch From Flatbush Avenue

Sixto shopping for a Christmas present for his son, Bobby, who turns seven next week. He walks into a sporting goods store on Flatbush Avenue and the owner keeps an eye on him as he tries on several baseball gloves. Sixto has already taken his son out to Ebbets Field to see the Dodgers and young Bobby becomes an ardent fan. This summer Jackie Robinson is on his way to Rookie of the Year honors and over the course of the next ten years the Dodgers are brilliant, led by Robinson, Reese, Hodges, Furillo, Erskine, Gilliam, Newcombe, and Snider.

No Latin players, no Puerto Ricans.

The first Puerto Rican baseball player to appear in the major leagues was a pitcher named Hiram Bithorn in 1942, whose actual last name was Sosa and of whom no one has ever heard of outside of Puerto Rico.

Dispatch From We Won't Come Back Till It's Over

Congress approved the Jones-Shafroth Act in 1917, which gave Puerto Ricans U.S. citizenship with certain limitations. This was convenient because shortly thereafter Congress passed the Selective Service Act so as to raise an army to fight the Germans.

Upward of 20,000 Puerto Ricans served in the U.S. Armed Forces during World War I and imagine that. Fighting for a commander-in-chief you had no voice in electing. That's how it was back then in 1917.

That's how it is now in 2023.

One such WWI soldier was a man named Rafael Hernández Marín, who went on to become a popular songwriter, penning hundreds of songs in all of the Puerto Rican styles, *canción*, *bolero*, and *guaracha*.

Hernández was working as a musician in North Carolina when the U.S. entered the war. Jazz bandleader James Reese Europe, predecessor to Duke Ellington and Count Basie, recruited Hernández and his brother, Jesús, and 16 other Puerto Ricans to join his Harlem Hellfighters outfit. They toured Europe with Europe's band throughout the war years. After the war, in the early '20s, Hernández moved to New York City and began writing songs.

My grandfather was too young to serve in WWI, but Jones-Shafroth did pave the way for him to migrate to Brooklyn.

I'd like to say that my grandfather played Hernández's music for me and my sister, but I have no memory of him ever playing us any Puerto Rican music. I'm certain he would've heard of Hernández, as he was a musician himself. There was the keyboard that stood off to the side of the living room and I think I remember him playing it, but not anything specific, and not anything Puerto Rican. Maybe he did and I was too young to recognize it.

My father sang doo-wop on the streets of Brooklyn and could always pick out sweet harmonies, but I don't know if he ever accompanied my grandfather.

I remember my father singing harmony to my rendition of "For the Good Times" by Kris Kristofferson one afternoon in the early 1990s. The song starts with the lyric "Don't look so sad, I know it's over" and devolves from there. I can still hear my father joining in on the chorus, unrehearsed and unplanned, "Lay your head upon my pillow."

I can only imagine Sixto like it is a movie, a young man arriving with a tattered valise in 1920s New York. He wouldn't have to check in at Ellis Island after Jones-Shafroth, so he was free to go anywhere. I don't know if he had a contact in the city, a friend or relative he could stay with while he looked for a place to live. I don't know why he chose Brooklyn instead of Manhattan or the Bronx. I don't know how he found a job, as a longshoreman, though maybe that was years later. Maybe he worked in restaurants, maybe he painted houses, maybe he busked on the street for loose change.

I can't imagine leaving my home to go live somewhere else, not even now.

I can't imagine going somewhere the people would think of me as second or third class, somewhere I'd be shunned and scorned.

That winter a few years ago I couldn't imagine leaving my home for almost anything.

Dispatch From Enping

I asked Cary Ng about his relationship to language and family history during the changeovers of our match. He said that while he speaks Cantonese at home with his family he cannot read or write it very well, having never studied it in school.

He said his wife, who is also Chinese, can't speak Cantonese or Mandarin at all.

I like knowing about other casualties of assimilation.

Cary is a relative newcomer to tennis. I started playing in earnest when I turned 40, in the wake of a failed relationship. I needed something to do and always liked the game and figured it was a better way to kill time than watching hours and hours of *Law & Order* and drinking bourbon and looking for trouble.

But I'm a level above Cary due to my background in baseball, proficiency from both wings and the serve. Cary has a good and consistent forehand, hits it with both pace and topspin, but only chips the backhand with a slice that doesn't have much action on it. The ball floats into my court and is easy to handle. Like a lot of amateurs or what commentators on TV call "club players," his second serve is weak, as he is only trying to get the ball into the box. As the returner I can either take control of the point right away or win it immediately.

I lose it immediately, too, and just as often, it seems.

As a former baseball player and part-time switch hitter, I showed up to tennis with a big two-fisted backhand. It's my stronger side, though I've worked hard to improve the forehand and I can now employ it as a weapon.

Inconsistency and footwork are my biggest problems and what keep me at a certain level. I make way too many unforced errors and get tired too easily and as a result stop moving my feet and then I hate myself. I can crush serves, both firsts and seconds, if I'm going after it like I should, but double-fault too often and then like so many of my friends I baby the second serve for fear of double-faulting but I keep double-faulting anyway and it makes me want to quit the sport forever.

I was a good hitter as a baseball player and it translates into tennis. However, hand-eye coordination and athletic ability don't help when it comes to the Spanish language.

Whenever I read Spanish I recognize a fair amount of words and can sometimes have a general idea of what's written. Maybe this is due to taking Spanish in junior high school or maybe it comes from a basic understanding of languages after a lifetime of reading.

Either way it's not enough and wholly inadequate.

Cary tells me that his family comes from a poor agrarian city in China called Enping and he says more than half of its residents have to move overseas to make a living and provide for their families. Cary said his great-grandfather worked in Cuba for 20 years, his grandfather did likewise in the Dominican Republic, and his parents in Puerto Rico. He has cousins that still live in Mexico.

I can't decide if this makes him more Latino than me.

I know it's my turn to tell Cary about my family history, the who what where why and when. Instead I talk about the ball toss and how we all need to improve our second serve.

What I could've said is—no one ever told me anything and I never asked.

It's the mirror I won't look into because I can't, because there's nothing to see.

All I can see is a typical American suburban childhood filled with Little League and fast food, MTV and senior prom, cruising the Pike in Ronnie's Camaro on Friday nights, doing absolutely nothing.

And maybe all that was fine and a dream fulfilled for someone back in Puerto Rico circa 1928, but maybe there was a way to do this while listening to "Oye Como Va" and eating *asopao*.

I do remember a joke my grandfather told me once, something about the national anthem at a baseball game and a little boy in the stands. The gist of it was *O, say, can you see*, and my grandfather altering it to, *Jose, can you see?* and Jose saying, yes, he could see just fine.

Dispatch From Vieques

Sixto on a raft with four strangers floating to Florida. They shoved off early this morning from a beach in Vieques when it was still dark. Sixto has one canteen full of water, some bread, dried pork, *plátanos*, and a guitar. Maybe halfway to landfall— no one knows for sure, as they don't have a compass or charts or maps—the raft capsizes. Sixto is in the process of drowning when one of the strangers, a man named Ernesto, swims over to Sixto and wrangles him back to the raft. They struggle to turn the raft right-side up but eventually they do and then they pull themselves up and into it. When Sixto regains his senses, he thanks Ernesto, who is still breathing heavily, and then they sit in silence as they realize the other three men are gone.

The next night Sixto finds his way to Calle Ocho and a vacant room in a flophouse. He sleeps for 14 hours straight without stirring. The next morning he hops a train to New York City.

The guitar didn't survive the trip, but he plans to get a new one just as soon as he lands a job, perhaps as a line cook or street hustler.

Dispatch From Number 42

I don't think my grandfather liked Jackie Robinson. He once told me that he saw Jackie grab his crotch in response to someone in the crowd harassing him.

I think he said this was classless.

I imagine there was more to it.

Dispatch From Clouds Drifting By

The only thing I remember about Puerto Rican Day Parades past were the attacks in 2000 when multiple assailants harassed, sexually assaulted, and robbed random people marching in or watching the parade. Many of these attacks were caught on video and over 50 women reported being assaulted.

The suspected ringleader of these attacks, which seemed methodical and premeditated, was a Dominican from Washington Heights, who was quoted by the press as saying he was just having fun.

Perhaps he was trying to give Puerto Ricans a bad name.

I didn't know this about the Puerto Rican Day Parade attacks, that those responsible weren't Puerto Ricans. I don't know why this should bring some sort of ex post facto relief to me, but it does.

I wonder if thinking myself a sham Puerto Rican is equivalent to a Black person not being "Black enough."

I was almost finished with the sandwich and turned down the Tito Puento so I could listen to the commentary on the parade. The hosts on ABC were an attractive rainbow of Puerto Ricans and they all had to speak loudly as sirens blared so they could introduce the official band of the parade led by conductor Papo Vázquez.

The rainbow consisted of four people, three men and one woman, and all different shades, ranging from fair to dark.

Dispatch From One Excuse After Another

I've been asked if I speak Spanish countless times and countless times I've said no, that I understand a little, *un poquito*, and that my father didn't speak Spanish, either, and my mother is Italian, so maybe let's shut the fuck up about it.

I don't know why this has gotten inside me now as opposed to years ago. Perhaps it's because I'm nearing 50, another year older and closer to death. Perhaps it's because we had a president that classified Mexicans as criminals and didn't know that Puerto Rico is part of the United States, sort of.

I suppose before I was busy or had other things on my mind.

My sister remembers our grandmother talking to her in Spanish and then telling her what she just said in English. She said she was an early teen, which means I was, as well.

I must've been outside playing ball or held hostage in a snow fort.

Or my sister is lying and can't be trusted.

My Italian grandparents were both born in New York City. Their parents were from Italy, a town called Roscigno, which is a name I didn't hear until I was in my 30s. One of my mother's 98 cousins compiled a cookbook and skeletal family history.

Dispatch From Fort Bliss And The French Riviera

The word *spicks* was first seen in print in *Scribner's Magazine* in 1916, as reported to describe the term border troops at Fort Bliss, just north of El Paso, had employed to describe Mexicans.

In F. Scott Fitzgerald's *Tender Is the Night*, one character describes another from Rome, an Italian presumably, with this exclamation... He's a spic!

I have never heard an Italian called a spic. Dago, guinea, wop, sure, but never spic.

Dispatch From Nassau County

I don't know if Sixto spoke English before he'd immigrated to New York City or if he learned it once he was living and working here. He always spoke with a thick accent and I always had a hard time understanding him, particularly on the phone when I was a child.

He died when I was 16 and his death meant almost nothing to me, other than what I felt for my father.

Dispatch From There'd Better Be A Good Reason

Sixto had three children, Gloria, Robert, and another whose name I don't know. She died as a child and my father never told us anything about his late sister.

My mother doesn't know the name of her late husband's sister, but thinks it was Maria. And my sister didn't even know that her father had another sister.

You'd think there was something to hide, some great shame.

Which is why I don't think Sixto was chased out of Puerto Rico for cuckolding a local gangster, the one he used to run numbers for, a corpulent man named Pedrocito.

Dispatch From September 12th

Next to me on a plane was a little boy and in his lap was a little girl, presumably his sister. The children played musical chairs before takeoff and continued throughout the flight. Their mother was in the aisle seat. She had a dark olive complexion, dark hair and eyes. She looked like me, which is to say she looked Puerto Rican. She wore a gaudy white baseball cap with rhinestones affixed to its face. She had on dark eyeliner and blue eye shadow and a big diamond ring on one hand and several rings on the other and a thick gold watch and thin gold bracelets and painted pink or mauve fingernails. If people still wear pearl earrings then she had a large one in her right ear. I couldn't see if she had one in her left, but I assumed she did. Her fingernails weren't long, but they weren't short. She was left-handed and filling out paperwork that was held together by the clipboard resting in her lap.

The little boy had her complexion, but the little girl did not.

Her husband, sitting in the same row on the other side of the aisle, was Jewish and wore a kippah. There were many Jewish men on this plane and all of them wore kippahs. They all cradled infants and had fathered several children each. They all wore polo shirts tucked into dark trousers, which revealed the same paunch, and most wore glasses. They walked up and down the aisles and exchanged words as they passed each other.

Only one had a wife who looked Puerto Rican.

Whenever I fly I think of September 11th. I was in Long Island City, Queens, that morning and stood on a rooftop and took pictures of the towers as they burned and subsequently fell to the ground. The following week on the subway every brown person kept their heads down out of fear or shame, as though they were responsible.

I never wondered what it might feel like to be the object of suspicion, to be feared for the color of your skin, your dress, your beard. Of course, brown people in this country have been ostracized and feared for hundreds of years, have been the target of violence and oppression, but I never got the sense that I'd been subjected to it, that I'd been singled out because I was Latino, though I'm sure I was.

I don't remember anyone ever clutching her purse as I walked by or crossing to the other side of the street, but maybe I missed it.

This is what happens when you lose identity, you don't think of yourself as other.

Dispatch From The Left Bank

I didn't care for my grandmother, which is probably why I'm not curious about her side of the family. If I don't feel a kinship with Puerto Rico or Puerto Ricans, I at least feel the absence of it.

But Cuba and Spain might as well be Haiti and Portugal or Mars and Jupiter.

My grandmother was someone who responded to her husband's whistle like she was a servant.

She wasn't mean-spirited, nor was she generous or warm. She was peculiar in a thoroughly uninteresting way.

When all of us were watching a ballgame on television and the camera panned the crowd she'd say, Look at all the people, and then chuckle.

That's basically all she ever said.

There's no there there, said Gertrude Stein.

I can only speculate as to my grandmother's education and whether or not she finished high school.

My maternal grandmother read books and did crossword puzzles, though I don't know anything about her education, either.

One probably shouldn't compare and contrast grandmothers.

I'm not sure if I ever felt sorry for her or if I feel sorry now.

My grandmother wouldn't sit in the front passenger side of a car because it was the death seat. Instead, my sister, her granddaughter, would take the seat while she remained safe in the back.

My sister would've been a teenager at the time, my grandmother in her 80s.

I doubt she realized the absurdity of this.

I could go further, but then there's empathy and causality and context, although perhaps it's too late for all of that.

It was a different time, a different place, a different culture.

I have sinned, Lord, but I have several excellent excuses, said Henry Fonda in one of his many film roles.

Stories are like icebergs and subways, most of it is beneath the surface, said Diego Goldstein, who ripped off what Hemingway theorized in the early 20th century.

The gender roles between my grandfather and grandmother were somewhat similar on the Italian side of the family. At the end of a Sunday dinner, all the men remained at the table while the women buzzed around the kitchen, doing the dishes, clearing the table, getting ready to serve the coffee and dessert.

I never saw any of the men whistle for the women. Still, the roles were established and immutable. The women waited on the men and the children.

The brilliant and groundbreaking television show *The Sopranos* demonstrated this more than once throughout the run of the series. *The Sopranos* depicted a rather typical Italian family in New Jersey, save for the father's role as a mob boss.

One telling scene had the daughter, Meadow, eating breakfast at the table while her mother, Carmela, emptied the dishwasher in the kitchen. After downing the remaining fruit juice, Meadow shakes her empty glass at her mother, a signal that she wants more, and her mother is to drop everything, go to the refrigerator, retrieve the fruit juice, cross over the kitchen into the dining room to refill her glass.

This was a maneuver I saw more than once growing up.

You know how to whistle, don't you ...? said Lauren Bacall.

Dispatch From Mallorca

That Nadal is the greatest tennis player from Spain is indisputable and I am partially descended from Spain, though this is not enough to make me a Nadal fan or a colonist. One of my great-grandparents was from Spain. I don't know if it was my grandmother's mother or father who was Spanish or when they immigrated to New York City, where she was born somewhere in the mid-1910s.

No one in our contingent of tennis players resembles Nadal. There are some players who run down ball after ball, impossible gets left and right, and there are others who hit with great lefty topspin like Saj, one of my longtime hitting partners. Saj is tall and lanky and can hit the hell out of a forehand and obliterate a first or second serve. One of my favorite sights is when a short ball sits up for him and he comes out of his shoes to hit it, often missing the baseline by several feet, sometimes hitting the back fence. But when he makes the shot it is Keatsian, a thing of beauty.

Can pronounces his name *John* and is an excellent player. He can flatten out his serve and blast it by you for an ace or spin it in and have it bounce well over your head. He is also an excellent athlete and chases down balls he has no right getting a racket on. He's young, in his 20s, so you have to marvel and pity him, for his boundless energy and what he's headed for in 20 years. The young guys never think they're going to get old.

I've been told I move well considering my age. I'm fast out there, even still, but everything hurts and just as often as not my legs feel heavy on the court. I play too much and I weigh too much and I don't see any of that changing.

Sunil speaks with a British accent and is talented but wildly inconsistent. His good shot to mistake ratio is probably 1:5. Jorge is a wisecracking bilingual architect, also a fine player and great ball-striker, but not at all nimble. Like me he is in his late 40s and has been hampered by injuries. Most recently it was a partially torn MCL. I was the one who hit the ball he was trying to get a racket on when his leg gave way underneath him and he crumpled to the ground.

Jorge makes too many mistakes trying to show off, look-away half volleys, ridiculous drop shots. He plays to the cameras even though there are no cameras.

I sometimes play to the cameras, too, with the same look-away half volleys and occasional forward-facing tweener. Maybe it's a Latin thing. Maybe that's my connection.

Dispatch From Who Might Be Watching

Every time the camera closed in on a Puerto Rican in the crowd or on a float, they felt obligated to wave and smile and shimmy. Some of the women wore revealing clothes, plunging necklines, short-shorts and skirts.

I switched back in time to see Nadal execute a perfect chip and charge, finishing the point at the net with a backhand drop volley.

My good shot to mistake ratio varies depending on the day. I'm more consistent than Sunil but that's only because I play more than he does. There are a slew of us who are always out there, hitting, drilling, playing groundstroke games, sets and ladder matches, singles and doubles.

Always I look around to see who might be watching. Maybe it's a future opponent in the ladder, maybe some of the better players, maybe a pretty woman.

I'm not as consistent as I'd like to be and there's no amount of work or practice that is going to change it. If you were a layman and you watched me out there you'd likely be impressed. I can smoke a serve upward of 105 miles per hour, maybe 110, can drill a fallaway cross-court forehand for a clean winner from behind the baseline, can hit a down-the-line two-fisted backhand that is poetry.

But those are only moments and while they are glorious, they are fleeting. There is always the next ball, the next shot. Those great shots sustain me out there, but there are countless mishits and framed volleys or overheads and abject laziness even though one of the reasons I'm out there is to get exercise. One thing you hear on the courts all the time is players admonishing themselves to move their feet. I am probably the most guilty of this in the whole Western Hemisphere and say this out loud about 20 times a session, along with another common rebuke, watch the ball.

The kid whose Trans-Am my father didn't let me buy, Kenny Ono, played Little League with me. His father, Mr. Ono, was a coach and you could always hear him yelling from the dugout, See the ball good.

I imagine it would be the same way if I were to learn Spanish. I would sound great with this sentence or that one and then like an imposter with the next. Anyone would be able to tell that I was faking it, that I didn't know what I was doing.

I like to think had I stayed with the ex-girlfriend who spoke Spanish that I would've picked up at least some Spanish, enough to be conversational, perhaps even pass as a real Latino. She talked of wanting to take me to Spain, so that was a missed opportunity, another loss. Total immersion would be the only way, though I know that's not true.

When I read Neruda to the ex-girlfriend in Spanish I'd pronounce maybe 70% of the words correctly, but I probably understood less than half.

Dispatch From Hibbing, MN

Sixto said he was homesick for Puerto Rico sometime during the last year or two of his life. I don't remember him ever talking about Puerto Rico or what he was homesick for. I don't know anything about Mayagüez other than what I've read on the Internet or in books.

Maybe it was the food or the weather or his family. Maybe it was the music or the beaches.

I don't know if he and my grandmother ever visited Puerto Rico once they'd moved to Brooklyn.

Democracy dies in darkness—*The Washington Post* said that.

Families die in silence—I said that.

Dispatch From One World Trade

I never wondered how it might've felt if Latinos took down the Twin Towers. It's one thing to be feared for snatching a purse, jacking a car, stealing hubcaps, but another for mass murder, for terrorism.

I felt awful that there were people around town wearing a button that said "I am a Sikh American" over or across a picture of the American flag because ignorant and racist Americans didn't know the difference between Sikhs and Arabs, not that it should matter in this particular instance.

Sikhs were afraid that they would be beaten and killed by angry white Americans out for revenge.

All brown people wearing something on their heads are threats or targets: turbans, keffiyeh headscarves, hooded sweatshirts, bandanas, kippahs, skullcaps.

Dispatch From Since I Was So Quickly Done For

My mother found out from one of my grandmother's cousins that the little girl who died, my father's older sister, was named Helen. According to this cousin, a woman named Fig Figueroa, she died at six from pneumonia. This would've been sometime in the late '30s or early '40s.

Dispatch From What You Can't Beat

I have another friend named Brian Kubarycz, who grew up Mormon and learned Spanish when he was a missionary in Argentina at the age of 20.

I'm sure I know other non-Latinos who speak Spanish, but for these purposes you can't beat a Chinese guy and a Mormon.

This is what I think about now. I think about language and history and people who can speak a language that for me should've been a birthright.

I also think about health quite a lot. The family history I do know, my grandfather's cancer, my father's cardiac arrhythmia, my mother's mini stroke, her weak aortic valve and amnesia.

I wound up in the ER once, thinking I was having a heart attack. I felt a tightness and general ugliness in my chest and figured this was it. It was 2007, ten years after my father died and 20 years after my grandfather. I remember thinking about the symmetry of it all, that my death would be poetic in some way.

Not much of what I keep in the medicine cabinet is supposed to help prevent heart attack or stroke. For that I eat a lot of oatmeal and play a lot of tennis and hope for the best.

I also hope to never experience these particular catastrophes or if I do, that they occur a long time from now and kill me off all at once.

Surviving seems fraught with a number of difficulties, not the least of which would be no more tennis. And for a stroke the potential loss of the only language I can traffic in, the only identity I have.

Language is identity, it's memory, it's history, it's everything, and it's nothing you can buy at the pharmacy.

And while language is in itself history it can't completely take the place of history, either; of the story I can tell about who I am and where I come from, the old longshoreman/boxer, the sanitation worker/singer, the local assimilated college professor done good.

If I could tell my story in Spanish to Jorge or Cary it might partially fill that void, that lack of narrative, but only to a degree.

Dispatch From The Squared Circle

Sixto as a welterweight in the Puerto Rican version of the Golden Gloves. He was known as a counterpuncher with a lightning-quick left jab. Toward the end of his career he fought Pedro Montañez, who was regarded as one of the most talented fighters to never win a world title and lost a title bout in the Polo Grounds to someone he'd previously defeated.

Sixto's record was 22-3 with 14 knockouts before he had to retire due to a detached retina. This is when he turned to music, though he enjoyed taking his son to the fights on Friday nights and watching boxing on television.

Maybe this is what he was homesick for not long before he died. He missed being inside the squared circle and practicing the sweet science in front of all the pretty girls. He missed putting the gloves on and pummeling his opponent with a torrent of body blows, lightning-quick combinations that were often indefensible.

I watched boxing with my father but can't remember the last time I had any interest in the sport.

Julio César Chávez, the Mexican champion considered one of the greatest boxers of all time, was our favorite. His match with Meldrick Taylor in 1990, garnering a technical knockout with only two seconds remaining in the 12th round, is still one of the greatest and most memorable sporting events I've ever seen.

I'm sure my grandfather would've been a fan of Chávez and maybe he was.

Or maybe he didn't like Mexicans.

Dispatch From See The Ball Good

What separates the best tennis players from everyone else is footwork. Watch the little steps they make to move their bodies into position to hit the ball perfectly. This is what I find nearly impossible to execute whenever I'm tired, which is almost all the time. I'll chase after a drop shot with vigor and urgency almost every time, or that ball labeled for the far corner, but I can't make myself take three small steps to hit the ball properly when my legs feel as though they weigh 200 pounds each. So I use my strong hand-eye coordination to hit some stupid-looking shot that works about half the time. I'll be caught off balance but manage to somehow pull my hands in close to my body to make decent contact.

This happened during a key moment of one doubles match. We were at 5-all and the third deuce on Can's serve when he hit a deep cross-court approach shot that tied me up, but I somehow hit a backhand winner up the line, even though I should've taken two or three tiny steps to hit a forehand. It looked stupid, but it worked and we wound up breaking to win the game.

One of the most beautiful and elegant sights is Roger Federer hitting any shot. He watches the ball contacting the strings every time, forehand, backhand, volleys. His eyes are still on the contact point for a solid second after the ball has been sent on its way to the other court. He doesn't pick his head up to see where the ball is going, he knows where it's going. He's making sure he keeps his head down and his eyes on the ball.

It seems so fundamental, yet I fail to do this all the time, on volleys especially. I'm too concerned with what's about to happen rather than what I need to do to get the desired result, a stark reminder that I'll never be as good as I want to be.

Dispatch From Puerto Nowhere

The hosts of the parade coverage had praised Senator Chuck Schumer's salsa moves as he paraded by the main staging area. They said something about rhythm, about style, but no one said he was good.

One of the hosts was Taíno, who are an indigenous people of the Caribbean. By the time the Europeans showed up in the late 15th century, the Taíno were the principal inhabitants of what are now Cuba, Hispaniola, Jamaica, the Bahamas, and Puerto Rico.

He was not quite as dark as the guys who worked in the kitchen.

I have to confess that I'd never heard of the Taíno before. I'm pretty good with history, but not this apparently.

The grand marshal of the parade was pop star Ricky Martin, who first became famous as part of the boy group from Puerto Rico called Menudo.

His big hit as a solo artist was the vapid "Livin' la Vida Loca."

This is what everyone is trying to do on television and on social media, live a crazy life. And they want you to know everything about it.

The very definition of a parade, from the cavemen right through to the Puerto Rican Day Parade.

There is one prominent Puerto Rican tennis player, Monica Puig, who won the gold medal in the 2016 Olympics in Rio de Janeiro, Brazil.

Her gold medal win was totally unexpected, as she's never been a top-ranked player and had never done particularly well in a major tournament. I like to watch her play because she's ferocious and hits the ball hard and always goes for her shots and she's good-looking. I also like that she's Puerto Rican and I root for her whenever she's on Tennis Channel.

Some of the parade marchers were wearing flamboyant and colorful costumes, replete with elaborate headdresses, presumably native to the island.

There was aerial footage of the Puerto Rican flag, which looked like it stretched out for a full city block as it was carried along Fifth Avenue.

All of the floats had people playing drums and dancing and waving flags.

One of the co-hosts, Sunny Hostin, was telling a story about the flag, how whenever her family moved into a new apartment the first thing they would do was hang the flag up somewhere, from a fire escape or window.

I never saw a Puerto Rican flag at my grandparents' in Brooklyn.

Dispatch From Something To Be

Here's a response to Brokaw's *Hispanics* comment: Indeed, one should make an effort to learn the local language, but not at the expense of your native tongue. Preserving one's culture and heritage is not only in the best interest of the immigrant, but it's what's best for America. Diversity is strength in every respect, including genetically. Diversity adds texture and flavor. One can't make a stew or soup from one ingredient.

I don't know if my grandparents thought about any of this when they were raising their children. If they considered the ramifications of what it means to assimilate, what it means to be a good American.

They didn't talk to therapists and guidance counselors about it. They didn't read books by sociologists or other academics on the importance of culture and identity.

It's what most working-class people did when they came to America in the first half of the 20th century. They worked, earned a living, provided for their families. No time for anything else.

I don't know if my father ever thought about these issues, either. I don't know if my father felt as though he'd lost some part of himself.

I'm pretty sure he didn't, though.

So, sure, we assimilated and it was successful, but here I am missing an arm.

Dispatch From Somewhere Other Than Florida

Before we took off the woman who looked Puerto Rican spoke Spanish while on the phone. But her Spanish was no good, she spoke it like a *gringa*. It sounded like she learned it in an American school, maybe one in Jersey.

Maybe she isn't Puerto Rican or maybe she's Puerto Rican like I am.

Perhaps I would've asked her if she'd been seated next to me, if there wasn't a child between us.

She had on a hooded sweatshirt, black spandex pants with a black skirt over it, and white sneakers that had some sort of gold emblem. It seemed as if she'd spent the past week lying on a beach somewhere, but we all boarded the plane in Newark.

We were maybe 10 or 15 minutes from landing. We were flying low to the ground and it felt like I could jump out without causing injury.

Below, Florida was a mosaic of highways and trees and bodies of water, some of which looked man-made.

That morning I started in Brooklyn, made my way to Manhattan and then Newark.

Then we landed and I was somewhere else, somewhere in Florida.

Dispatch From The Unthinkable

The love I had for the members of my immediate family, father, mother, sister, was profound, deep, and superstitious when I was a kid. I was always afraid that something was going to happen to my parents, that they'd get killed off in a car accident. I'd have to say *be careful* to them on their way out the door otherwise they'd wreck and my sister and I would be orphans.

I had to have been scarred by a movie or television show I'd seen as a child. Which is why I always had to make sure that any fights or quarrels were resolved before anyone left the house. The guilt that the character or characters lived with afterward seemed oppressive and unthinkable.

My mother is also neurotic, the neuroticism bequeathed to her from her own mother, so it is somewhat genetic.

I'd line up for a corner jumper at the basketball courts in the park across the street from my house. I'd say *this is so everyone in my family will be okay* and let it fly. If I missed the shot I'd take another, repeating the same line. I couldn't leave until I made the shot and saved my family. I'd do this when disposing of paper in a wastebasket, as well.

I suppose this was an obsessive compulsion, like Nadal blessing and fondling himself on the court. The difference, of course, is I was trying to save lives and no one ever saw me do it.

But this love and insanity didn't extend beyond the immediate family, the nuclear family, which was a term that confused me for years as a child.

I never worried about my grandparents. I never feared losing them, never looked forward to seeing them.

I would've been fine with my grandmother taking her chances in the front passenger seat instead of my sister.

This might have nothing to do with assimilation or something to do with it or it might speak to who they were as people, though you probably can't separate any of this.

Of course, not all assimilated Americans feel this way about their grandparents, if they were the ones who perpetrated the assimilation.

I saw that my father respected his father, but only tolerated his mother. He never said it out loud, of course, but we all knew. His relationship to her was obligatory, particularly after my grandfather died. My father was always big on obligation and never shirked any sort of responsibility.

My father died ten years after his father did, on August 29, 1997, two days before my own 26th birthday.

I spent most of 2007 keeping an eye out for falling safes.

Don't die before you're dead, said Yevgeny Yevtushenko.

Dispatch From North Of The Equator

I've never traveled to a Spanish-speaking country. Part of the reason is I feel awful in hot weather and all of Latin America is too close to the equator for my taste. Another reason is I'd have to apologize and say I don't understand, I don't speak Spanish, all the time and who needs that.

I don't have any children now and don't plan on having any in the future. I won't have to worry over what to tell my child about her last name, what to tell him about our ancestors from the island, how come we don't speak the language.

All of it dies with me.

Dispatch From Flushing, Queens

The parade coverage ran for three and a half hours. I don't know how it's possible anyone can watch for that long, either on television or in person.

I made myself another sandwich but decided to save it for another time.

Much like almost everything else, it's the same thing over and over. People dancing, waving flags, smiling and laughing, music and noise, hitting the ball over the net so that the other player can do likewise, over and again, ad infinitauseum.

Menudo y menudo y pues nada y pues nada.

The hosts were running out of things to talk about and this is when they called for a biopic on Roberto Clemente, the first great Puerto Rican baseball star.

Which reminded me that the Mets were also playing, so I changed the channel to watch them take on the Colorado Rockies. The Mets were thoroughly mediocre that season, like me as a tennis player.

Mediocrity can have several definitions but for me it's moments of absolute brilliance followed by moments of what the actual fuck.

The middling and mediocre third basemen, Todd Frazier, lifetime .241 hitter, managed to get enough of a slow-breaking curveball to hit it over the wall for a three-run homer in the first inning and that was all the Mets needed on that day. Their putrid bullpen didn't blow the lead as they had in so many games that season.

As for Frazier, he rarely looked good in the batter's box. He was often off balance, his top hand flying off the bat as a result, and he was forever flailing at the ball. This occurred on his first inning home run, too, which was only possible due to the irrefutable truth that the ball was juiced. There were a record number of home runs hit that season and some of them looked ridiculous. Routine pop flies kept carrying and carrying until they cleared the fence.

It's likely MLB officials arranged for the balls to be more tightly wound in an effort to boost sagging attendance and television ratings, though commissioner Rob Manfred denied this.

Home runs are a spectacle and this is what they want. Small ball, nuanced fundamentals like hitting behind runners and bunting have all but disappeared in today's game. The announcers, who are often older than me, bemoan this as much as I do.

So there was Frazier out front on a pitch yet again, weight on his left foot, a bad position to hit the ball hard. But he kept his hands back and flicked the bat at the ball as it approached the plate and somehow it worked, somehow the ball left the yard. Frazier himself looked surprised and the pitcher cursed himself and the laws of physics and the announcers were once again stupefied as the ball sailed through the air in a lazy arc, landing three rows deep into the half-empty bleachers.

Dispatch From The Western, Semi-Western, Continental

Maybe I'd have a better forehand if I spoke Spanish.

Now I spend time thinking about connections and missed connections. I think about how this country drew millions of people to it who were willing to relinquish so much of who and what they were.

I think about an alternate reality where I did grow up speaking Spanish. I think how it might've changed me; how it might've pushed me beyond the narrow quarters of the world I've spent all of my life within. Maybe I'd fly to a literary conference in Chile instead of Florida, maybe I'd translate books to Spanish or write one myself in the language.

I think about the vague sense of rootlessness I've always felt, a niggling yet permanent disconnect.

Latinos do look at those of us who don't speak the language as suspect. Maybe this attitude isn't as prevalent over time, as one develops either professional or personal relationships, but it's always there in the background.

It's as if we should have some sort of scarlet letter embroidered into our clothing, perhaps an *I* for Ignoramus or rather, *Ignorante.*

Or an *F* for Fake—*Falso.*

Dispatch From JoJo And Sweet Loretta Martin

The reading at UCF was a good time. One measures success in these instances by the audience, do they seem at all interested, engaged. The students, both under and over graduates, were warm and welcoming and asked questions I've answered a hundred times before, but such is the life of a traveling con artist.

I signed a lot of books for students after the event, which is always a nice thing to do, a good feeling to enjoy for a few minutes before the bitterness and ennui kicks back in.

One such student, a young woman named Rulanda, said she made a bad decision in the name of literature in buying my most recent novel. She said she was broke, but went ahead and bought the book anyway.

It never occurred to me that my grandparents didn't have any money, but clearly they were poor. They lived in Starrett City, public housing, in a one-bedroom apartment. They didn't own a car or go on any vacations.

One year I got a birthday card from my grandmother with a five-dollar bill taped inside it and the words *I AM BROKE* written between the closing and signature.

We didn't have money or go on vacations, either, except for the occasional trip to Amish Country in Lancaster, Pennsylvania.

We would eat at restaurants called Good 'N Plenty or Plain & Fancy. When I was 14 and my sister 12 my parents took us to Disney World in Florida. All I can remember from that trip was setting the North American record for cursing while riding on the Space Mountain roller coaster.

But my parents kept us fed and we had our own bedrooms with air conditioning and downstairs there was cable television and in the driveway were two modest but reliable cars. We never went without and we never went anywhere else.

Now at the age of 50 I finally make a decent living as a full-time professor at Stony Brook University. I get paid much more to talk about writing and books than my grandfather made on the docks or my father made on his routes.

Dispatch From Now You Go Too Far

The reading at the bar in Florida had featured four readers and seven or eight audience members, which is a terrible ratio, but typical. The first reader, a young woman named Ashley, had to contend with the loud and mindless conversation of the bar patrons who were not there for the reading, but to get their drink on and perhaps find their way into someone's pants. Finally, Holly, the friend who organized the event, went over to say something and there could've been a donnybrook and at such point decisions would've had to be made.

I always used to fantasize about bar fights and justifiable homicide. Some fraternity types going too far and me having to put them down.

I had no choice, officer, Chad and his brother Todd there had gone too far.

Of course, the officer would side with Chad and Todd because he too wears polo shirts tucked into cargo shorts, set off with boat shoes and ball caps, is both violent and racist, and I'd be the one led off in handcuffs and leg irons.

That is if I wasn't shot in the face before the arrest because I look like someone named Robert Lopez.

Dispatch From A-Hun-Twenty-Fifth Street

Two days later and I was on a plane back home from Orlando. The overnight bag was lighter by only a few books because one was sold the night of the first reading, another was sold on the way to the airport, and I gave one or two away to lighten the load. The bag was still too heavy.

The plane was populated by all manner of brown peoples, with the occasional white family coming back from Disney, presumably, mixed in for balance or ballast.

One of the flight attendants spoke English with a thick Spanish accent, but he didn't sound like my grandfather. After he made a few routine announcements he then said the same in Spanish. I'm not sure if this is the first time I've heard this on a domestic flight.

The night of the bar reading I met a man who told me a story about his father, how he used to smuggle marijuana from Colombia with his brother, who wound up getting busted with ten tons of weed. The brother was a disbarred lawyer and got off on an illegal search-and-seizure loophole. Years later this man at the reading was trying to get a job with the NSA and had to be investigated by the FBI, which is standard procedure. His father called him one day and asked, Why the fuck are you sending cops to my door? Naturally, the father didn't cooperate and the man had to convince his father to go talk to them so he could get the security clearance he needed.

I've always been envious of people who could tell stories like this about their families.

In the movie version of my story Sixto finds his way to Brooklyn and walks the streets, not knowing exactly what to do with himself. He finds his way into a saloon and meets a young tough who asks if he can leave something with him, a leather satchel. Sixto takes the satchel home to the studio apartment he's sharing with a friend but doesn't look inside of it, doesn't want to know what this young tough is mixed up in.

In real life I don't know what happened. The Great Depression would start soon, within a few years of his arrival, but I have no idea how this affected him.

The economy was already in a downturn before 1929 and many Puerto Ricans found themselves competing with other ethnic groups for all kinds of unskilled labor. The "Harlem Riots" of 1926 featured unemployed Puerto Ricans squaring off against unemployed Jews.

The *Jewish Daily Bulletin* report on July 28, 1926, had an "advance guard of the Porto Rican army" that planned to attack the Jews with long sticks and bricks.

I like how they were called Porto Ricans, the way most *gringos* pronounce it.

When one does a Google search for *Harlem Riots* there are entries for 1919, 1926, 1935, 1943, 1964, 1968.

Sixto was in New York City during this time, but I've no idea where or if he even knew about these problems in Harlem.

My father read three daily newspapers so maybe he got that habit from Sixto. Maybe Sixto read about the riots in the *Herald* or the *World* or the *News* or the *Post*.

The *Herald* was staunchly anti-immigrant. The publisher, James Gordon Bennett Sr., reportedly said a newspaper's role is not to instruct, but to startle.

Maybe Sixto read the *Herald* to see what he was up against.

Dispatch From Luke The Drifter

I've been telling people about my seasonal affective disorder and there are plenty who think they have it, too. I think getting older has something to do with it. I'm tired almost all the time now and there's nothing out there for me anymore. Others agree, say the same thing.

Sometimes we recommend to each other something called light therapy boxes.

People who live closer to the equator do not suffer from seasonal affective disorder nearly as much as those who live farther away from the equator. It stands to reason seasonal affective disorder isn't much of a problem in Puerto Rico.

Dispatch From Your Future Address

For years I was petrified that something would happen to my father. He had high blood pressure but wasn't one for self-destruction at all. He hardly ever drank and quit smoking in the early '70s. He was athletic and stocky, not overweight or unhealthy. He loved food and could eat, but that was his only vice.

Still, even as a child, I'd linger in the hallway after going to the bathroom in the middle of the night. I had to hear the sound of him breathing while he slept before I could go back to bed.

I never talked to him about what it meant to be Puerto Rican. He never brought it up and I never asked.

I wish now that I had asked him if he'd ever been called a spic. But, this was the '70s and '80s and we were father and son. We didn't discuss such things.

In the wake of my father's death I'd visit his grave every week. I did this for at least a year or two. I remember the feeling of seeing the temporary marker replaced by the headstone, probably a month or two after the funeral. Seeing his name, the same as mine, Robert Lopez, on a grave. How it somehow made it official and permanent.

I've only been to the cemetery once in the last ten years, as I live in Brooklyn and he's buried on Long Island and I didn't own a car until very recently. But I imagine that even if I did live closer I'd visit his grave infrequently, perhaps once a year, on his birthday.

This is what happens over time. You get used to the loss and absence. You don't visit cemeteries and don't practice the same superstitions. You don't speak the language you spoke as a child.

When I say you I mean me, like I often do. But I'm sure it applies to other people, too.

I haven't been to my grandfather's grave since his funeral and I have no memory of that particular cemetery. I remember his wake, hugging my father and seeing his eyes well up, but never spill over. My grandmother was a sort of zombie right up until the last hour of the second day of viewing, when she finally broke down and wept.

I'm planning to go out to the cemetery in a couple of weekends. I'll look at Sixto Lopez's grave. Maybe I'll say something out loud. Maybe I'll tell him that I turned out to be a college professor and am writing about him now, that the United States was attacked with airplanes by terrorists, that a moronic fascist fraud was elected president and the Mets still haven't won a World Series since 1986. Perhaps I'll say something about my sister and father, too.

The only Spanish I can remember my father speaking was when he'd recall his time in Panama, serving in the army. He was there in November 1963 and went on high alert after President Kennedy was assassinated in Dallas on the 22nd.

Language is the only homeland, Czesław Miłosz is quoted as saying.

My father would mimic one of his Southern comrades while they were out on the town, invoking a colorful drawl, *No hablo español, señorita.*

Me neither, s*eñorita.*

Me neither.

Dispatch From Harness Your Blame

My grandfather did make rice and beans and I think my father had a Tito Puente record or two, so there was that.

According to two Pew Research Center national surveys, researchers found that about half of second-generation self-identified Latinos are bilingual. But language abilities diminish across generations: Among third or higher generation self-identified Latinos, fewer than a quarter are bilingual.

This forfeiting of the language, it's something that happens, like forgetting one day of your life for no reason at all.

Like imagining over and over having a stroke or heart attack. Like playing tennis with a Spanish-speaking Chinese guy or drinking beers with a multilingual Mormon. Like a medicine cabinet with a mirror inside a mirror.

There's no mention in the study if these Latinos know their family histories or if those had been eradicated as well.

Learning a language at 48 or 50 seems pretty much impossible.

In Bon Iver's song "The Wolves (Act I and II)" there's a lyric: What might've been lost don't bother me.

It's clear from Vernon's delivery of the line that this isn't at all true. There's an insistence to the refrain and layering of ethereal vocals, a constant cutting off and starting up, these repetitive loops along with a swell of additional voices, some in harmony, others in unison, that constitute a powerful chorus of abject denial.

What might've been lost don't bother me, either, except when I meet a Sanchez or Gonzalez or when someone asks me about my heritage or when I make myself rice and beans or when I'm alone and get to thinking.

Dispatch From North Brooklyn

With the outbreak of World War II, when millions of Americans were involved with the war effort, there was a sudden and great need to fill the jobs left behind, propelling the Great Migration from Puerto Rico. Puerto Ricans, both male and female, found employment in factories and ship docks, producing all manner of domestic and military hardware.

By the 1950s Puerto Rican neighborhoods, aka barrios, began forming in Williamsburg and Bushwick in Brooklyn, the South Bronx, Spanish Harlem, and the Lower East Side.

I think Sixto and his family lived in Red Hook, Brooklyn, during this time, maybe in the Red Hook houses.

In *When I Was Puerto Rican*, Esmeralda Santiago describes her experience in Williamsburg and Bushwick, two adjacent neighborhoods in Brooklyn, after her family migrated in the early '60s:

> There were two kinds of Puerto Ricans in school: the newly arrived, like myself, and the ones born in Brooklyn of Puerto Rican parents. The two types didn't mix. The Brooklyn Puerto Ricans spoke English, and often no Spanish at all. To them, Puerto Rico was the place where their grandparents lived, a place they visited on school and summer vacations,

a place which they complained was backward and mosquito-ridden.

By this time my father was in his early 20s and probably in the army. So he wouldn't have met young Esmeralda, but he was one of them, one that spoke no Spanish at all.

I don't remember my father ever mentioning his grandparents, though I assume they lived the rest of their lives in Puerto Rico. I don't know if he ever met them. He never mentioned visiting the island, so he probably didn't complain that it was backward and mosquito-ridden.

I know that my mother visited Puerto Rico, but this was before she met my father. And she's Italian, so there's that, too.

Dispatch From I Wasn't Looking

The first Puerto Rican Day Parade was held in Manhattan in April 1958.

The parade was organized as a celebration of Puerto Rican pride and is a tradition that not only continues today in New York City but is also practiced in other cities such as Chicago and Orlando.

According to the 2010 census, New York has the highest population of Puerto Rican residents, followed by Florida and New Jersey.

I didn't see any Puerto Ricans in Orlando during my visit, but I also wasn't looking.

I don't know if anyone saw one in me.

Dispatch From The Same Old Song

"I Don't Think the Cop is My Friend" is the title of a *New York Times* article from March 29, 1964, concerning the problems Puerto Ricans had with police at the time.

Back then Puerto Ricans objected to the police brutalizing and killing them.

According to the piece, "tensions erupted into violence last November on Manhattan's West Side after two Puerto Ricans, Victor Rodriguez and Maximo Salero, were shot to death by a policeman in a radio car. The police were taking the men to a station house for booking on a charge of disorderly conduct. They allege that Rodriguez shot at them from the back seat, and that they reacted in self-defense. Scores of Puerto Ricans and sympathizers thought otherwise. They picketed the station house to protest the killings, and marched down Broadway, stopping traffic, in a mood described as ugly and near-riotous."

One wonders how a man in the back seat of a police car had access to a gun. Maybe cops didn't frisk people they'd arrested in the 1960s.

While this case was in front of a grand jury, another young Puerto Rican named Francisco Rodriguez Jr. was shot dead by an off-duty policeman who said that "Rodriguez had slashed his jacket with a knife when he tried to end a scuffle."

Another piece from the *Times* about the Rodriguez killing stated that the off-duty cop was in a bar while the 18-year-old Rodriguez was involved in an altercation with a few other people outside the bar on the sidewalk. The off-duty cop intervened and then shot and killed Rodriguez as he was running away.

Over 300 people showed up for Rodriguez's funeral in what was described as a "combined funeral procession and protest."

A Puerto Rican lawyer said at the time, "Even though we come here as American citizens, many policemen look on us as aliens."

I doubt Sixto was one of the protestors but I'm sure plenty saw him as an alien, probably neighbors and colleagues, at least. I don't know if he ever had any run-ins with the police.

I didn't know him well enough to say that he was the type to get into a fight outside a bar. I'm not even sure what that type is or if there is such a type.

I can say the same about my father, the same for me.

These killings happened in Manhattan and while they were reported in the papers there's no way to know if Sixto or my father heard about it or what they thought.

My guess is they probably thought those Puerto Ricans did something wrong, that they had it coming.

I don't know if Sixto knew anyone who was murdered, let alone by police. The same goes for my father, although his brother-in-law was shot and killed in a bar in the Bronx in 1973.

But that was the Italian side of the family, so maybe that doesn't count.

My parents and teachers on Long Island taught me to trust the police. Law and order and public service and duty to one's community comprised the backbone of this country.

Dispatch From Madison, WI

Paulie Heenan is the only friend I've had who was murdered by police. He was killed on a late Thursday night in Madison, Wisconsin, in 2012.

I remember the first time I played tennis after Paulie was shot. We had to play late in the day, as we couldn't secure a court for the morning or early afternoon.

I play a lot of tennis and it's always the same. It feels great to hit a passing shot while falling away at the baseline and awful when I hustle up to the net to retrieve a drop shot and push it wide.

That first time playing tennis after Paulie was murdered, I kept thinking about him after every rally. Imagining the unimaginable scene. The reality of it, what actually happened, not how it might be rendered in a story or essay or film or play. The sound of shots fired in the wee hours of a suburban-like Wisconsin neighborhood. Residents waking to that sound, rushing to kitchen windows to look outside, then spilling out into the street. The cop with the gun in his hand vibrating with adrenaline, with elation, maybe even glee, the neighbor on the ground cowering in fear and horror.

I try not to think about Paulie bleeding out on the ground, dying.

Then back to cross-court forehands and down-the-line backhands and wondering how anyone can think Paulie a threat, regardless of circumstance. Knowing the cop had to think of himself as a cowboy, as a king-shit movie character.

Absolutely knowing this murderer, this police officer, like so many of his brethren across this country, thinks he's in a video game or a movie.

I relayed what had happened to Paulie to all my hitting partners for weeks afterward while we were warming up. I felt like I had to tell them, had to tell everyone.

Here is a mixture of fact and assertion—Paulie was a white guy, tall and skinny as fuck, gentle-hearted and a pacifist, bright and immensely talented, kind, generous. All of what people say when the victim is the last person you ever thought could get murdered by police.

But the truth is the cops can kill anybody. They do it all the time.

I can say that Paulie worked as a record producer and sound engineer and was out scouting bands on a Thursday night. He'd recently moved back home to Wisconsin from Brooklyn and was crashing with friends while looking for his own place and trying to regain his footing in a life he'd thought he'd left behind for good. Brooklyn wasn't going to be home for him and he knew it and he probably belonged in the woods doing his own thing, making music, rebuilding computers.

I can say that I met Paulie through his wife, Mae, who was my student at Pratt Institute. I can say that Mae is brilliant, a math and science geek with a gift for language. In class I'd mentioned that my computer, a Dell PC, had been compromised. I'd caught the virus, the malware. Mae said her boyfriend was a whiz and could fix it right up.

I can say that Paulie came over and cleaned out my computer and it took all day, about seven hours from start to finish. He explained how computer viruses work, how they are spread and team up to make a network of supercomputers. I pretended to understand what he was talking about. I can't remember what else we talked about during that time, but we covered quite a lot, particularly music. We made plans.

I can say that if Paulie allowed me to give him any money it was a token amount and only after I insisted. The second time he spent a whole day cleaning out my computer he refused what I offered and accepted lunch and dinner instead.

I can say that Paulie and Mae had me over for dinner once or twice.

I can say that I have a Mac now because Paulie said I should switch and the prospect of him rescuing my PC over and over, of taking advantage of his kindness and friendship, wasn't at all appealing.

I can say that after a long night of loud rock and booze on the night of November 8, 2012, Paulie, inebriated and exhausted, accidentally went into the wrong house. All of the houses on the block looked the same and he'd only just started crashing with his friends that week.

The homeowners called 911 when they heard someone downstairs. The man of the house recognized the intruder as Paulie, the young man who was staying with the neighbors next door, and walked him outside, as Paulie was quite impaired and needed assistance. This is when the cop pulled up, never identifying himself as a police officer, called for everyone to get on the ground, and drew his weapon. Paulie stumbled toward the cop, said something like, *Want to get weird*, and the cop shot him three times. The neighbor on the ground was calling out, *It's okay, he's my neighbor,* as it happened. The neighbor said Paulie was moving away from the cop when he was shot.

The cop said Paulie reached for his gun because of course.

I can say that I won't mention the cop's name because why should I, because it doesn't matter.

Mae wrote to me several months after the shooting and said, *I don't know anyone else who lost a person when another person decided to kill him. I think it's different than when people die in any other way. And it's vastly different between you and me, your father and Paulie, but I wonder how much the thing they have in common weighs.*

The weight Mae refers to here is hard to measure.

The expression that there is nothing to express, nothing with which to express, nothing from which to express, no power to express, no desire to express, together with the obligation to express, said Samuel Beckett.

That's how it is with everything I've managed to write, how it is when it comes to Paulie.

How it is when it comes to cops killing people. Like George Floyd, like Eric Garner, like Philando Castile, and like and like and like and like.

Who's gonna protect me from you? The likes of you? The nerve of you? said Gil Scott-Heron.

Playing tennis after a friend dies in this manner is strange. Like everything was strange after my father died suddenly two days before my 26th birthday in 1997. Eating meals, talking to my mother or sister, going back to graduate school, anything at all quotidian, all of it felt grotesque somehow, senseless, and profoundly wrong.

Everything in the world felt different, the sun up in the everywhere sky, watching a baseball game on television, listening to music, breathing.

One difference is my father died and Paulie was killed.

Another difference is my father's death leveled me in every way and I'm still trying to figure out how Paulie's murder has impacted me.

Of course, for Paulie's family, for his closest friends, for Mae, it's another story entirely.

Nothing to express and an obligation to express.

While driving through rural Georgia in the fall of 2016 with my closest friend, a tall blond-headed middle-aged white man named Sam, he joked that my presence in the car was going to get us killed. A cop was going to pull us over and we'd all wind up on the news that night.

I sometimes forget that people think of me as brown or non-white. I sometimes forget that my school-aged friends used to call me a spic.

Once I asked my friend Amanda, who was complaining about dating white men, if she thought of me as white or non-white. She said she'd never considered me white.

I remember coming across an article in *The Rumpus* titled "We Are Many, We Are Everywhere," and going through the names of a long list of writers of color, arranged by first name. As

I moved from the A's down through the alphabet and approached the R's it occurred to me… I'm going to be on this list.

And there I was, sandwiched between Rita Dove and Rochita Loenen-Ruiz.

Of course, being Latin and presenting as somewhat white, at least to most people, affords one this sort of luxury. Black men and women never forget they're Black, not in this country.

So here I was, a potential mortal liability to Sam while driving through Georgia.

Stories of cops brutalizing and killing people fall in and out of fashion. Why one instance becomes a cause célèbre and another doesn't has to do with chance and what else is going on in the world and the particular kind of narrative surrounding the killing. This is what sells newspapers, gets ratings, but why one killing and not another always feels capricious more than anything else.

Of course, having the violence caught on video changes everything. See Rodney King, George Floyd, Philando Castile.

I can and have imagined my life ending in a car accident or some sort of cardiac catastrophe, but getting shot and killed is unimaginable—even though my name is Robert Lopez and my complexion is a little darker and I have the shaved head and dark eyes and full lips and am built like a fire hydrant.

I thought this especially true, that we were courting some kind of potential danger, when Sam wanted to stop and get out of the car to touch the cotton as we passed through a sequence of cotton and pecan farms. I made sure to stay inside the car, certain that some overseer somewhere was taking aim through a telescopic lens.

Turns out I can imagine the unimaginable.

Everybody has got to die, but I have always believed an exception would be made in my case, said William Saroyan.

One of my tennis partners is a friend who shares a name with a man who four cops fired 41 bullets into in the Bronx in February 1999. He's a good player and a better guy, a freelance journalist who often writes about technology for *Forbes* and *The New York Times*.

You can get killed just for living in your American skin, said Bruce Springsteen.

Tennis is almost always a respite from the real world, one of its many blessings, but it wasn't that first time after Paulie's death.

Such is the weight of grief and trauma.

Sit still… til they remember how your boy was killed, said Patricia Smith.

I can say that Paulie and I played music together, recorded a few demos, and promised to do more of it. He was a whiz who could play all the instruments and had the technical expertise all recording engineers possess. He and I talked about making an album together in Wisconsin once he got settled.

He'd lent me some CDs before he'd moved back home, including a special edition of the Beach Boys' *Pet Sounds*, which all engineers and producers geek out on. I wanted to mail them back to him and I finally did and the package arrived two days after he was killed. Now when I type this, that Paulie was killed, it doesn't seem quite as fucked up and perverted, though, of course, it's still fucked up and perverted.

Such is the nature of time and familiarity.

Since Paulie was killed in November of 2012, police in this country have fatally shot over 10,000 people, but that's for another essay, a different movie.

Paulie wrote me an email a month before the shooting, said: *I've crashed and burned in Wisconsin, but if you're up for mailing those CDs to me I'd appreciate it. If not, no big deal. Hope to see you on the flipside, brother. I'm back to being a musician again.*

When I listen to the two songs we recorded together I especially dig the sweet fills of Paulie's guitar, him playing exactly what was needed to enhance the vocals, the emotion.

Now when I think about Paulie when I'm out on the courts it's in the context of how to write about his death, not who he was as a person, as a musician, as a friend. This is what gets lost over time or what can get lost if we're not careful.

But even if we are careful we inevitably lose the humanity of those lost. This is perhaps the greatest tragedy of being a person in the world, that we all become a story for someone else to tell until no one is left to tell it firsthand, if it's told at all.

It's the same with my father and grandfather, other relatives and friends, students and acquaintances, with everyone I know who isn't here anymore, everyone who has changed tense.

The stories of my grandfather are so thin and unsatisfying they're probably not worth telling. Flimsy anecdotes that don't at all speak to who he was or what he may've wanted out of life, what he wanted for his son, his grandchildren.

It's a shame, but maybe also a blessing. Maybe if I knew more about him I'd feel compelled to keep it to myself.

It's impossible to maintain history once everyone is gone and when no one wrote anything down. There's no record I can read through to learn about Sixto.

No one wrote or saved letters, no one kept a diary or journal.

I think my mother has some photographs of Sixto and Delores, but I haven't seen them in years.

And we turn him into an anecdote to dine out on ... But it was an experience ... How do we fit what happened to us ... without turning it into an anecdote... And we become these human juke boxes spilling out these anecdotes. ... How do we *keep* the experience? said John Guare.

That first time I played tennis after Paulie was shot, I remember that it was windy, and at that time of year with the sun hanging low in the sky, it was hard to see the ball coming in and out of the shadows.

Dispatch From Salt Lake City

One month before the pandemic shut the world down, I got to visit the University of Utah as a guest writer. I gave a reading, did a Q&A, had dinner one night and lunch the next day with graduate students and faculty, and met with several PhD students about their manuscripts. I read the manuscripts on the plane and had something valuable to say about two of them, offered something like hope to another, and asked a lot of questions for the last one.

I spent the week in an apartment in a residential neighborhood located not far from the university in Salt Lake City, Utah.

I received the invitation about 18 months before, which is how far in advance most of these gigs are planned. It always seems as far off as the next Olympics, the next presidential election, the next time something good might happen.

I've done this sort of thing many times all over the country. I've visited schools alone and have gone on week-long tours with my friend and fellow author, Sam, maybe half a dozen times. But it's only recently I've realized that universities can check off a box when I'm invited to be a visiting or guest writer. I'm the Latino writer for the semester.

This is a running theme, not realizing how I was or am perceived or what became obvious only in retrospect—that my grandparents were poor, that Long Island was a wasteland, that I was called a spic but never equated that with being Puerto Rican because why would I.

So, there I was, the short Latino on campus.

This isn't a condemnation of such a practice, as representation and diversity are good and I'm all for it, particularly when I'm the one they're inviting.

I'm not what some of them expected, I'm sure. Certainly, the director of the program, a friend of mine, was familiar with my work, so he knew there wasn't going to be any mention of barrios, gangs, poor immigrants sneaking into the country. There's no Spanglish in anything I'd written. There's never anything of what the corporate literary world demands of a Latino literary writer.

Most of what I've scribbled concerns people doing people things. Often the people don't even have names, let alone a skin color or ethnicity.

I'm a con man of sorts, the would-be Latino grifter coming to a half-empty auditorium or bookstore near you.

This was a business trip and I was all about business that week. I had no plans to visit with friends or see any sites, though I was curious about the Salt Lake and would've liked to have seen it before I left. I've heard it's a big dead thing and nothing at all to look at. I've heard that you shouldn't go out of your way to see it. I've heard that dead birds litter the shoreline.

In early 2008 there was something of a bird apocalypse and some 15,000 gulls, ducks, and grebes died at the lake from avian cholera.

I learned that it's the largest salt-water lake in the Western Hemisphere. I appreciate lakes that look and move like oceans.

I enjoy the idea of greatness in a lake, the grandeur of it. I like it when you can't see the entire lake from the shore, how the lake water stretches into the horizon and out of sight. It activates the imagination in a way that looking across the East River from downtown Brooklyn into Manhattan doesn't.

I enjoy looking upon Lake Michigan whenever I'm in Chicago. I like that they have a small ocean in the middle of a cosmopolitan city, it's good design.

Dispatch From Salt Lake City, Continued

Snowcapped mountains and hills surround the university. I felt like I was standing in the middle of a postcard, that I could've posed for a picture while clad in a snowsuit and holding a pair of skis. Exhaust fumes from my breath hung in the air upon exhalation. It is beautiful there, stunning even, but far too dry both indoors and out. I want to call it arid, but it was February and cold and I'm not sure anything can be called arid in the cold.

My eyes burned and it hurt to blink and my throat was in even worse shape. One morning I had the university procure a humidifier for me. I watched the steam rise into the air and disappear at eye level. I'm not sure it did any good, but I ran it ceaselessly for the entire week.

I bought eye drops and lip balm and applied each almost hourly but my eyes remained sandpits and my lips were a disaster. I thought about my grandfather and father working outside in the winter, in the elements. I used to enjoy playing touch football in the cold weather as a kid, particularly while it snowed. And I play tennis if the mercury reaches 40 degrees and when I first started playing anything above freezing meant it was go-time, but all that's fun. Otherwise, I don't want to be uncomfortable or inconvenienced even for a minute and so many things bother me.

But this was a skate compared to being in the hold and loading and unloading crates of bananas or whiskey.

I got to stay in a nice apartment and look out the window where I could see the porch next door and watch icicles melt in the late afternoon sunlight.

Dispatch From DeKalb Avenue

One afternoon in Brooklyn I was walking to lunch and thought I'd heard someone call my name behind me. I had over an hour to kill before my next class and figured I could use the walk and could use lunch and by the end of both it might be time for class again. So much of life is deciding how to kill time so that it's good and dead and doesn't Lazarus its way back to haunt you later.

Time is always a problem but so are the people who time makes a mess out of day by day and year by year.

I used to go home between classes but I'd moved recently, into my girlfriend's Park Slope apartment, and so going home wasn't an option. There wasn't time to go home, although I gamed it out and maybe getting to spend 20 minutes at home was worth the hassle of finding parking, which often included driving around the block once or twice and cutting down two different side streets. So the reward was I got to eat lunch and waste 20 glorious minutes, which wasn't enough time to get partially undressed and somewhat comfortable, but at least I wouldn't be subjected to other people. But then I'd have to drive back to campus and find parking there, which was the same drill without the side street Easter-egg hunt and so the upshot was fuck it all to hell.

This was all before Covid and quarantine. Like everyone else I stayed home to teach and didn't have to park the car unless it was to shuffle it from one side of the street to the other on Monday or Thursday depending on the side. You'd think this would be easy to remember, but I got the tickets to prove you wrong.

I always like going home best or I did when I used to leave the house. Almost anytime I left the house what I looked forward to most was returning. I used to find myself rushing home even if I didn't have anything I needed to do once I arrived there. My pace would quicken to the point where I could feel the lactic acid building and burning in my legs.

During the Covid quarantine the only time I left the house was for tennis or to shop for groceries.

Dispatch From The World Spins Too Fast

I always eat too fast, every meal. It's always disappointing, as I am constantly reminding myself to slow down and enjoy. When I say constantly, I mean once or twice a year. When I say too fast, I mean like how lightning skates across the sky too fast.

This is the antithesis of how my grandfather conducted himself at the table. Somehow, he made it seem like art. To this day I've never seen anyone eat like him.

I think I attributed this practice to his advanced age. I thought all old people ate this slowly, although I don't think my grandmother matched him. She seemed to finish at the same time as the rest of us.

My grandfather seemed to do everything at glacial speed, walking from one room to another, formulating a sentence to speak out loud.

I've never written about my grandfather before and I hadn't even thought of him that much. Maybe he would come to mind two or three times a year and almost always in conversation, some anecdote about my slipshod heritage.

I'd never actually thought about him, not in any real sense. Never wondered what his life was like, what he wanted from the world, from the mainland, for his children, his grandchildren, me.

Sixto lived till 83, but I don't see myself making it that far. The world spins too fast for me.

I make a dinner plan and I play tennis the next day and teach a class and watch the Rangers and I don't follow up on the dinner plan and neither does anyone else and then I play tennis and teach a class and watch the Rangers again and again and then two months go by and no one mentions the forgotten dinner or aborted plan. One day it snows and the next it's 70 degrees and the fruit stand on the corner was a diner two days ago and the day before that was a bodega and I'm walking along on the sidewalk and everything is fine, but then I get dizzy from the blaring sun and the pot smoke and the earth's ceaseless rotation and the ground turns into a fresh sheet of ice underneath my boots.

I was thinking about Sixto and time and there I was in Salt Lake City, Utah, over 3,000 miles from Puerto Rico.

This is why I told myself to slow down in a mediocre Italian restaurant, which was a short walk from the apartment.

Not long after the entrée arrived something happened that I'd only seen in the movies. A waiter with a faux Italian accent stood up in the middle of the dining room and sang a verse and chorus of "O Sole Mio" for the party of three he was serving.

This is when I signaled for the check and quickly finished the last of the chicken marsala over penne.

I could still hear him singing, *Sta 'nfronte a te* as I was walking out the door. He had a lovely tenor voice and everyone applauded when he finished.

Dispatch From Something Irretrievable

Sixto alone in his apartment in Brooklyn. He is 76 years old and can't remember the last time he picked up the guitar leaning against a corner in the living room. He gently strums a few chords, A minor into G, then F and E, back and forth. He plays with his fingers and slowly rakes his thumb across all six strings so that each note resonates and lingers until they make a single unified sound. This is how he tries to spark memory. He drastically slows the process so that something irretrievable can somehow present itself in the silence between tones, but he can't think of a song to play. He changes key and plays a C minor chord and then a G, which he recognizes as the intro to a song he played with Puente. He tries to visualize Tito out front on the bandstand, playing the timbales, standing up so he could cue the band and dance at the same time. Sixto is about to find the opening lyric when the neighbor's dog starts barking at the superintendent, who is knocking on everyone's door to check on a reported gas leak.

Dispatch From It's Now Or Never

Over the course of three days and nights the icicles melted. In between I gave a reading in an art gallery with a New York poet and did a Q&A over lunch as faculty and students sat around a table and talked about writing and no one asked questions about my heritage or the subject matter through an ethnic lens even though one faculty member kept on calling me Roberto at dinner afterward. I didn't correct her. I've had a few friends over the years call me Roberto, but they all knew my name was Robert. I don't think this woman, a middle-aged white poet, did. My friend Brian, the ex-Mormon who speaks Spanish, attended the reading and Q&A, but I didn't get much of a chance to speak with him. This is always how it works when there are too many people in a room. The conversation over lunch was all about craft and the writer's life and so I didn't have to say anything about being a LINO. Later that night I sat in the apartment with the humidifier on full blast and applied eye drops and chapstick while I read and worked and watched the icicles drip down and disappear.

Dispatch From Everyone A Hazard

The person who called out to me when I was walking to lunch was a colleague and also between classes. We've played tennis together, so we share something like a bond. He's one of the very few players who hit two-fisted on both forehand and backhand, like Mario. His groundstrokes are consistent and he hits with pace and heavy topspin.

We walked and talked for two or three blocks, as we hadn't seen each other in a while. He was on sabbatical for a year and I felt good about remembering this and asking him about it. He told me what he'd worked on during his sabbatical and I told him what I'd worked on during his sabbatical and we made a plan to have lunch the following week. We said we'd email each other.

By the following week no one had emailed anyone about lunch or anything else.

The truth is I would've liked to have lunch with my friend and colleague and I'm sure he also wanted lunch but we'd fallen into a habit of saying let's get together for a drink or for a hit and that one of us was dying to play and it'd be great to catch up but then time would fly by like one of Nadal's passing shots.

Then there was the pandemic and the subsequent lockdown and quarantine and the long overdue uprising that seemed to affect some real change across the country, at least for a while, at least in some ways.

Everything was different, including how we made plans and experienced time.

I still rushed home and in the early days of quarantine, this was understandable, encouraged even.

Outside everyone was a terrorist, everyone a biological hazard.

I threatened to make a backyard plan with another friend, drinks but probably not food and maybe even BYOB, but like so many plans to make plans, no actual dates were ever suggested and nothing ever came of it.

A plan to make a plan is what exactly?

Is it that everyone I know is old and tired and when it comes right down to it staying at home is easier than leaving the house even though we all have other intentions? We all want to spend time together and it always sounds like a good idea at the time but in the end we'd rather spend time at home alone.

This feels like the road to hell and how it's paved and what Lyle Lovett said in one song: It's just a fact of life that no one cares to mention, she wasn't good but she had good intentions.

I take a certain amount of solace in these plans to make plans, even though that and $2.75 and a mask will get you on the subway these days.

Assimilating in a foreign land is easier than maintaining one's cultural practices, less hassle with neighbors and strangers and employers and bigots and white people.

Maybe Sixto took the easy way out, did what everyone else in his community was doing.

Maybe he intended to at least teach his children the Spanish language but something always got in the way, a 48-hour shift at the docks, a world war, a month-long tour with Puente, something good on TV like the Dodgers winning the World Series in 1955.

Dispatch From That's The Way It Was

I don't know when my grandmother died. We lost track of her shortly after my father died in 1997. My mother said that she moved to Florida to live with my aunt Gloria, but I don't know how she came to know that.

My mother would call the cemetery where my grandfather is buried, St. Charles in Farmingdale, New York, every so often to see if Lola had checked in next to him. She did this for years until she stopped.

I'm not sure how she learned of her mother-in-law's death, but she relayed the information to me through instant message.

Everyone knew that we had no real ties to her, no emotional investment. But she was still my grandmother. I said something like that to my mom. I said, you just told me my grandmother died via instant messenger.

It felt disrespectful, yet somehow appropriate.

Dispatch From Vilnius

Vitas Gerulaitis won a men's doubles championship at Wimbledon and a singles title at the Australian Open.

He died in 1994 at the age of 40 from carbon monoxide poisoning while sleeping in a friend's guesthouse in Southampton, New York.

He was born in Brooklyn to Lithuanian parents and is buried in the same cemetery as my grandparents.

I have no plans to visit his grave when I eventually do visit my grandfather's, which I've been threatening to do for three years now, but I remember when Gerulaitis died and feeling awful about it.

Vitas gave the greatest quote of all time after finally besting Jimmy Connors in 1980: Nobody beats Vitas Gerulaitis 17 times in a row.

Vitas Gerulaitis. Further proof that the world is a beautiful and rotten place.

Dispatch From Don't Call Me Saint Peter

I can't imagine playing tennis in Salt Lake City. It feels like my lungs would burn on the thin, desiccated air.

Every day I was there and not back home was a day of tennis I'll never get back.

Dispatch From The Sociology Department

I'm sure my colleague and I would've talked about how one of us is a Black man and the other is halfway Latino and how our mostly white students were on the right side of the protests against systemic racism and the police murdering people. So many of them took to the streets themselves, so many posted on social media every day. We would've talked about how great they are while pointing out what's troubling about the institution's student population and the obvious dearth of Black and Latino students.

Maybe it's because it's an arts school and only rich white kids are either interested or can afford to be interested in such follies. Maybe spending four years and hundreds of thousands of dollars studying negative space and character development isn't a good idea.

Maybe it's good that young Black and brown people are at other colleges, studying other disciplines. Maybe they'll make money someday and get to exploit other people because this is America.

Maybe money is the only path to change, either as individuals or as a society.

We wouldn't have any answers because there aren't any, but it would've felt good to hear each other talk about this.

I imagine Sixto came here from Puerto Rico because he had little choice, because everyone he knew was doing likewise, because if he ever wanted a life of if not prosperity, per se, then one tier above abject poverty, it had to happen in the States, in New York.

But he never made much money as a longshoreman and I think Delores may've worked as a cashier and so they both died poor. My father never made much money as a sanitation worker and I haven't made much money as a university professor, at least not yet.

I'm not sure I would've talked about this with my friend and colleague. Instead, we might've discussed time and how it moves.

Maybe we'd both say that after a while this pandemic and quarantining wasn't that bad and maybe this means that people can get used to anything. Maybe it means that a lot of us were already waiting for the world to end and it turned out to be as boring as everything else, like sitting at a window and watching an icicle melt in the sun, which I didn't think was boring at the time.

The trouble with the end of the world is what to do the day after.

Dispatch From Gates Avenue

The trouble with keeping plans is I like eating meals alone. In this way I'm like my grandfather.

Maybe this is the only trait I share with Sixto. Maybe music, too, and perhaps a love for baseball.

When I dine alone I think about changing my grip on the forehand and the unforced errors I made in my last match and my grandfather's *arroz con chuletas* and what the Rangers need to do to improve like developing their prospects and getting rid of plodding defensemen.

Now that I'm 50 I think about comfort and the home Jenny and I have made together. How it feels like I've arrived somewhere I wasn't trying to get to until recently. Years ago, I never thought or cared about living in a nicer apartment with tons of space and light. I didn't think about indoor trees and houseplants and accent chairs and throw rugs and tapestries to hang on the walls. Back then I had my head down and was writing a lot of fiction and teaching lots of classes and dating lots of women and playing lots of tennis. Back then I was all, I don't care too much for money, money can't buy me love, and now I think about a house somewhere in the country and retirement and how long I'll keep teaching and that I probably won't ever retire because I won't be able to afford it. I started too late with the making of the money so that's the price I'll have to pay and such is life in Puerto Nowhere.

I never thought about that kind of future because I was too busy in the present. Perhaps this myopia is where I deviate from Sixto and my father. They broke their backs their entire lives and my life is somehow their reward, is what they achieved.

It's probably not enough.

Survival is the best billions of people can hope for and the very idea of upward mobility is for a scant and lucky few.

Maybe I saw myself as someone who had to survive and thus couldn't afford to think about the future. Maybe my father dying at 56 had something to do with it, as well.

I don't always get this heavy when I eat alone at a restaurant by myself, but I always think about going home and how I can kill the rest of the day once I get there.

Dispatch From Salt Lake City, Continued

When you think of Utah you think white people. You think Mormons.

That was my expectation and it was thoroughly met. There were some brown people here and there on campus, but it's not that surprising as the university has a massive population and draws students from all over the world.

I hadn't been surrounded by that many white people since living on Long Island.

In the apartment there was a ledge directly over the bed. It had a few random books on it, a puzzle, and a pretty plastic flower in a bud vase.

I thought it was nice that someone had gone to the trouble of putting a fresh flower out for a stranger. I found myself leaning in to smell it but turns out it was plastic.

I'd never been offended by plastic flowers, what with their immortality and lack of pollen, but I was a little disappointed.

I've always suffered from allergies, which is only further proof that human life on this planet is some kind of cosmic joke, a grand mistake. That people get sick from flowers, trees, and grass is both hilarious and perverse.

To draw the obvious parallel, I'm the plastic flower as the token Latino writer for the semester.

Maybe this institution does a great job with diversity and representation vis-à-vis guest writers, as most colleges and universities are hyper-aware of these issues today.

Maybe when the faculty assembles syllabi it's like Noah and the Ark, we need our Native American Writer and our Asian Writer and our Black Writer and our Latina Writer and our Gay Writer and our Trans Writer and our Physically Challenged Writer and our Non-Binary Writer and our Black Trans Half Asian Physically Challenged Native American Writer, which is what we all do now and it's both ridiculous and appropriate.

I'm not sure if one thinks of racists, per se, when one thinks of Utah or if predominantly white populations are inherently racist.

Where are all the brown people, one could ask. Were they here once and driven out via gentrification or a Trail of Tears death march or have they been shut out altogether?

It's easier to vilify and demonize a people when there are none around.

Dispatch From Portland, OR

I lived in Oregon for about 15 minutes, but managed to finish a novel and a marriage there. I enjoyed the food and natural beauty, but didn't mix with people.

Oregon has a history of codified racism. The region's provisional government passed a law excluding Black people from the territory in 1844.

In the 1920s, Oregon had the largest chapter of the Ku Klux Klan west of the Mississippi.

Oregon didn't re-ratify the 14th Amendment, adopted in 1868, which guaranteed equal protection of the laws and citizenship to all born or naturalized in the United States, including former enslaved people, until 1973.

The obsolete language from the old law excluding Black people from Oregon wasn't removed from the state constitution until 2002. Even then, over a quarter of voters cast their ballot against the removal.

Oregon and Utah feel like neighbors, both spiritually and geographically, but Nevada and Idaho are in the way.

According to the 2010 U.S. census, less than 2% of Utah's population is Black, less than 3% Asian. Latinos/Latinas, which the

U.S. government still refers to as Hispanics, comprise almost 13% of the population.

I didn't see one Latin-looking person.

Dispatch From The Bathroom Sink

There were ants in the bathroom sink of my Salt Lake City apartment. I also found them on the tile above the sink, on the mirror, inside the medicine cabinet, on the tile of the shower ledge, on the floor, one or two in the living room, and a lone straggler in the kitchen. I was killing them all week.

The 45th president of the Unites States said once, "Democrats… don't care about crime and want illegal immigrants, no matter how bad they may be, to pour into and infest our country."

He said Baltimore, "… is a disgusting, rat and rodent infested mess." He instructed four Congresswomen to go back and help fix the totally broken and crime infested places from which they came.

The 45th president and various members of his administration appeared unaware that Puerto Rico is part of the United States. Certainly he doesn't think Puerto Rico should be part of the United States. He said, in the wake of Hurricane Maria, that the island's "incompetent" and "corrupt" politicians "only take from USA" and that Puerto Rico would "continue to hurt our Farmers and States with these massive payments."

He also wanted to sell Puerto Rico after the hurricane, which devastated the island and killed an estimated 3,000 U.S. citizens.

The staggering ignorance is the natural progression from Reagan to Bush Jr. to Palin to the 45th president. Disengaged, dense, clueless, and every ugliness manifested into one vile and worthless human being.

You know the 45th president thinks of Puerto Rico as infested.

I wrote the manager of the rental apartment and informed him of the ant infestation the day after I'd arrived. He offered to come over and take care of it, but I didn't want to have to contend with chemicals on top of the dry air, which I still hadn't gotten used to.

It's possible he would've used traps instead, but this didn't occur to me when I refused his offer.

I'm skeptical of a spray that can kill ants but is otherwise harmless.

Whenever I sleep in a hotel or guest room I think about Vitas Gerulaitis.

Late one afternoon I decided to check out the bathroom. I took a thorough census and there were 11 ants moving about the tub in no discernible formation.

I decided not to do anything about it that time.

Dispatch From A Better Moment

I had lunch one day with my friend Molly and on our way to the restaurant we drove past the Salt Lake Temple, which was the only sight I saw while in town.

According to the Internet, Brigham Young was the one who marked its location in 1847, which I believe means he decided where it should be built. The site was dedicated on February 14, 1853, which was exactly 167 years to the day of my passing it in a 2010 Nissan Versa.

Driving by at around 35 miles an hour I can say that the temple is impressive. There are spires.

I've seen similar spires on churches and cathedrals in other cities, including my own.

The Shoshone, Ute, and Paiute had lived in the Salt Lake Valley for thousands of years before the Mormons showed up.

Apparently they were all skiing in Park City when Brigham Young arrived in Salt Lake City and found it empty.

I had no real plans to go see the lake, though Molly did take me to the university campus to climb some stairs near the library. Once there we stood on a bench and Molly pointed out where the lake was hiding in the distance. Apparently, a tiny sliver of it is visible between the branches of a far-off tree line and one's imagination.

It's like standing in the exact right spot in Brooklyn Heights with a good pair of binoculars and trying to see Puerto Rico.

I think maybe I saw a sliver of the lake or I said I did to make it a better moment.

Dispatch From An Opportunity Lost

I could've stolen a motorcycle last year, but I was running late to tennis that morning so there wasn't time.

Also, I don't know how to operate a motorcycle.

Sixto never learned how to drive a car like a lot of denizens of New York City. My father used to drive to Brooklyn to pick up my grandparents and then drive them back to our house on Long Island so they could visit.

I did think about stealing the motorcycle because it was right there in front of Jenny's apartment, running with the keys in the ignition. No one was minding it, no one was around.

I thought perhaps I should've stolen it, keeping in mind Canada Bill Jones' maxim, It's immoral to let a sucker keep his money.

Substitute *motorcycle* for *money* and it's almost the same logic.

This was in Park Slope and so you know the owner of the motorcycle had it coming, too.

I'm not sure what I would've done with the motorcycle or where I would've gone so I'm not sure it's in any way logical.

Maybe if my grandmother were there she would've ratted me out, but maybe only if I was planning the theft in Spanish with an accomplice.

I don't even ride a bicycle, which in Brooklyn puts me in the minority, or so it seems. Most of my tennis friends ride and they tell me I should get myself a bicycle, that it would make my life easier. Meaning it would make going to and from the courts easier, which is pretty much the only place I need to go.

Canada Bill Jones was famed as a con man and card sharp in the late 19th century and considered by historians to be the very best in the world, particularly at three-card monte.

I used to practice cheating at cards with my friend John when we were teenagers. We'd seen *The Sting* about 45 times, featuring Paul Newman and Robert Redford, and this was going to be our calling.

Three-card monte is a relative of the shell game, where you have to keep your eye on the Queen of Hearts or the tiny ball underneath the three shells.

By the time the hustler finishes his machinations you only think you know where the Queen or tiny ball is on the table.

This fascination with crime is due to all the movies and television shows I watched as a kid growing up in the '70s and '80s. I also imagine that being a New Yorker had something to do with it, that being Puerto Rican and Italian had something to do with it, too.

Puerto Ricans stole hubcaps and cars and wielded switchblades. Italians ran numbers and protection rackets and carried guns. Much better to be Italian, according to *West Side Story* and *The Godfather*, *12 Angry Men*, and *GoodFellas*.

I imagine it's because crime seems easy and doesn't seem to involve real work. I've never wanted to do real work in the world, like what my father and grandfather had to do, working for the city in the Department of Sanitation or for what I assume were mobsters as a longshoreman.

I don't like waking up in the morning and having to go do something, unless it's tennis.

Sixto playing "Speak Softly Love" on the keyboard. My father and I trading lines of dialogue from *The Godfather*.

I'm my own variety of American con man. The fraudulent Latino universities keep hiring to prove they embrace diversity and representation.

Maybe anyone who calls themselves an American is a con artist, regardless of when their ancestors got here.

Stealing a motorcycle with the keys in the ignition seems easy, but the rest is more like keeping your eye on the Queen in three-card monte. After the frenetic shuffling you're absolutely sure she's on the left, but there goes your spirit and money when it turns out the Queen was in the middle or on the right or maybe the Queen was a Jack or a King or never there at all.

Dispatch From Puerto Nowhere

The plan all along was to go to Puerto Rico and look for my grandfather on the streets of Mayagüez, but the pandemic put a temporary restraining order on it. I'd wanted to imagine where Sixto might've gone to school, played ball, worked in a cantina. I'd talk to strangers and ask the questions I should've asked my grandfather. I'd visit libraries and government buildings like Alex Haley did in the 1960s when he first started tracing his roots. I'd hope to find long-lost dead relatives, read their names in a yellowed ledger.

I'd go to San Juan because it seems you must even though I don't particularly like cities anymore and maybe Ponce and a beach like Pelicano or Flamenco even though I don't enjoy beaches.

I'd speak English and carry a Spanish dictionary with me and hope for the best.

I'd hope to feel something.

I'd hope to eat *mofongo* and *pernil* and *arroz y habichuelas* and listen to some *bolero*.

I still want to go to Puerto Rico.

Meanwhile, I finally made it out to see Sixto in St. Charles Cemetery.

I had a faculty retreat to attend in Southampton, so Farmingdale was on the way.

His grave's location is listed as 016—NN-141.

Acknowledgements

Grateful acknowledgement to the editors of the publications in which some of these words first appeared, most in very different forms.

Big thanks to Sam Ligon for the many thoughtful reads of the many drafts of this book.

Big thanks to my family, as always.

Massive thanks to Eric and Eliza Obenauf, a bona fide dream team, for seeing what this book could be and having the patience, tenacity, brilliance, and a dozen more superlatives, at least, to help make it so. This book was a collaborative effort.

Notes

Page 4: *I pity the poor immigrant when his gladness comes to pass*: Bob Dylan, "I Pity the Poor Immigrant," *John Wesley Harding* (Columbia Records, 1967).

Page 16: *No iron spike can pierce a human heart as icily as a period in the right place*: Isaac Babel, translated by Peter Constantine, "Guy de Maupassant," *The Collected Stories of Isaac Babel* (W.W. Norton, 2002).

Page 19: *When a writer is born into a family the family is finished*: quote attributed to Czesław Miłosz: Peter Crawley, "If you're from a family of writers, everything is fair game," *The Irish Times*, Oct. 3, 2017; Retrieved Dec. 24, 2022, from https://www.irishtimes.com/culture/if-you-re-from-a-family-of-writers-everything-is-fair-game-1.3240983.

Page 22: *Much have I traveled in the realms of gold*: John Keats, "On First Looking Into Chapman's Homer," *The Poems of John Keats*, edited by E. de Sélincourt (Dodd, Mead and Company, 1905).

Page 27: *According to a Morning Consult-New York Times poll conducted in 2017 in the wake of Hurricane Maria, almost half of Americans didn't realize Puerto Rico is a U.S. territory*: Kyle Dropp and Brendan Nyhan, "Nearly Half of Americans Don't Know Puerto Ricans Are Fellow Citizens," *The New York Times*, Sept. 26, 2017; Retrieved Dec 24, 2022, from https://www.nytimes.com/2017/09/26/upshot/nearly-half-of-americans-dont-know-people-in-puerto-ricoans-are-fellow-citizens.html.

Page 27: *Since 1898, Congress has debated 101 bills related to citizenship in Puerto Rico and enacted 11 overlapping citizenship laws*: Charles R. Venator-Santiago, "Are Puerto Ricans American Citizens?" *U.S. News*, March 3, 2017; Retrieved Aug. 14, 2022, from https://www.usnews.com/news/national-news/articles/2017-03-03/are-puerto-ricans-american-citizens.

Page 27: *Puerto Ricans pay the same payroll taxes as mainland Americans, but don't get the same Social Security or Medicaid benefits*: Susan Milligan, "A Territory in Limbo," *U.S. News*, June 8, 2018; Retrieved Dec. 24, 2022, from https://www.usnews.com/

news/the-report/articles/2018-06-08/puerto-ricans-are-americans-but-they-dont-get-all-the-benefits.

Page 27: *Puerto Rico is the land that democratic theory forgot*: Luis Fuentes-Rohwer, "The Land that Democratic Theory Forgot," *Indiana Law Journal*, Vol. 83: Iss. 4, Article 13, Fall 2008; Retrieved Aug. 14, 2022, from https://ilj.law.indiana.edu/articles/83/83_4_FuentesRohwer.pdf.

Page 29: *In January 2022, federal prosecutors filed seditious conspiracy charges against the leader of the far-right organization the Oath Keepers and ten other individuals for their role in the January 6, 2021, attack on the U.S. Capitol*: "Leader of Oath Keepers and 10 Other Individuals Indicted in Federal Court for Seditious Conspiracy and Other Offenses Related to U.S. Capitol Breach," Department of Justice, Jan. 13, 2022; Retrieved Dec. 24, 2022, from https://www.justice.gov/opa/pr/leader-oath-keepers-and-10-other-individuals-indicted-federal-court-seditious-conspiracy-and.

Page 29: *four armed Puerto Rican nationalists opened fire on members of the U.S. Congress in 1954*: "Timeline of 1954 Shooting Events," *History, Art & Archives, U.S. House of Representatives*; Retrieved Dec. 24, 2022, from https://history.house.gov/Exhibitions-and-Publications/1954-Shooting/Essays/Timeline/.

Page 29: *two Puerto Rican nationalists tried to assassinate President Truman in 1950*: Andrew Glass, "Puerto Rican militants try to assassinate Truman, Nov. 1, 1950," *Politico*, Nov. 1, 2017; Retrieved Dec. 24, 2022, from https://www.politico.com/story/2017/11/01/puerto-rican-militants-try-to-assassinate-truman-nov-1-1950-244323.

Page 29: María Luisa Paúl, "The rare sedition charge filed against oath keepers was used before - against Puerto Rican nationalists," *The Washington Post*, Jan. 16, 2022; Retrieved Aug. 14, 2022, from https://www.washingtonpost.com/history/2022/01/15/seditious-conspiracy-charges.

Page 31: *Lopez is the 12th most common surname in the country, with about 874,500 people sharing the name, according to the 2010 U.S. census*: "Frequently Occurring Surnames from the 2010 Census"; Retrieved Dec. 24, 2022, from https://www.census.gov/topics/population/genealogy/data/2010_surnames.html.

Page 32: *Fragments are the only forms I trust*: Donald Barthelme, "See the Moon?" *Sixty Stories* (Penguin Books, 2003).

Page 32: *We tell stories in order to live*: Joan Didion, *The White Album*, (Simon & Schuster, 1979).

Page 34: *As if you could kill time without injuring eternity*: Henry David Thoreau, *Walden* (Thomas Y. Crowell & Company, 1910).

Page 44: *Transient global amnesia*: Mayo Clinic; Retrieved Aug. 14, 2022, from https://www.mayoclinic.org/diseases-conditions/transient-global-amnesia/symptoms-causes/syc-20378531.

Pages 72–3: Bruce Nelson, *Divided We Stand: American Workers and the Struggle for Black Equality* (Princeton University Press, 2001).

Page 75: *Dutch colonists established the village of Roode Hoek in 1636*: Michelle Montalbano, "A (Not So) Brief History of Red Hook," Brooklyn Public Library, Sept. 10, 2019; Retrieved Dec. 24, 2022, from https://www.bklynlibrary.org/blog/2019/09/10/not-so-brief-history-red.

Page 75: *the Lenape, an indigenous people of what would become New York, Delaware, New Jersey, and Pennsylvania*: Lenape Nation of PA, https://www.lenape-nation.org/.

Page 75: *From the time the Atlantic Basin was dredged and opened around 1850, right up until technology changed everything over 100 years later, Red Hook's ports were some of the busiest in the country*: "Erie Canal Boats: building bigger and bigger, 1817-1899," The Red Hook WaterStories; Retrieved Dec. 24, 2022, from https://redhookwaterstories.org/items/show/1643.

Page 75: *H.P. Lovecraft lived in Red Hook and wrote a horror story about it*: The H.P. Lovecraft Historical Society, https://www.hplhs.org/darthrh.php.

Page 75: *Hubert Selby Jr. lived close to Red Hook and wrote Last Exit to Brooklyn, published in 1964, about the dockworkers and seamy underbelly of Brooklyn's waterfront*: Henry Stewart, "Fifty Years Later, Looking for Last Exit,'" *Bklynr*, Oct. 10, 2014; Retrieved Dec. 24, 2022, from https://www.bklynr.com/fifty-years-later-looking-for-last-exit/.

Page 76: *Arthur Miller's A View from the Bridge deals with the corruption of the docks*: Arthur Miller, *A View from the Bridge* (Penguin Classics, 2009).

Page 76: *as does On the Waterfront, which was set in Red Hook*: On the Waterfront, directed by Elia Kazan, written by Budd Schulberg (Columbia Pictures Corporation, 1954).

Page 76: *The Red Hook Houses were completed in 1939 for the growing number of dockworkers*: "A (Not So) Brief History of Red Hook," Brooklyn Public Library.

Page 76: *More than 20,000 were thought to live in Red Hook at various points over the next 20 years. Today it's the largest housing project in Brooklyn*: Waterfront Museum; Retrieved Dec. 24, 2022, from https://waterfrontmuseum.org/red-hook-history.

Page 77: *King of the streets, child of clay, Joey, Joey, what made them want to come and blow you away*: Bob Dylan, "Joey," *Desire* (Columbia Records, 1976).

Page 83: *The world is not my home I'm just a-passing through*: Co-written by Tom Waits and Kathleen Brennan, "Come On Up to the House," *Mule Variations* (ANTI-, 1999).

Page 85: *where I was born, early Lord one frosty morn*: Sung by Elvis Presley, "An American Trilogy," *As Recorded at Madison Square Garden* (RCA Records, 1972).

Page 87: Coral Murphy Marcos and Patricia Mazzei, "The Rush for a Slice of Paradise in Puerto Rico," *The New York Times*, Jan. 31, 2022; Retrieved Aug. 14, 2022, from https://www.nytimes.com/2022/01/31/us/puerto-rico-gentrification.html.

Page 87: Ibid; *It feels like Hurricane Maria placed a 'For Sale' sign on the island*: Gloria Cuevas Viera.

Page 98: *Families are always rising and falling in America*: Spoken by Leonardo Di-Caprio in the role of Billy Costigan in *The Departed*, directed by Martin Scorsese and written by William Monahan (Warner Bros., 2006).

Page 100: *From the beginning Starrett City housed individuals on the basis of an affirmative action program wherein 70% of households went to non-Hispanic white families and the other 30% to minority families. In 1976, those minority households were 19% Black, 9% Hispanic, and 2% Asian*: Joseph P. Fried, "People Move In, And Starrett City Is Homey at Last," *The New York Times*, May 23, 1976; Retrieved Dec. 24, 2022, from https://www.nytimes.com/1976/05/23/archives/people-move-in-and-starrett-city-is-homey-at-last-as-people-move-in.html.

Page 100: *By 1979 the proportion of white residents declined to 64%. At the time advertisements for Starrett City featured testimonials from mostly white residents, but applicants were far more often non-white than white*: Michael Goodwin, "Starrett City Lone Concern: Rent," *The New York Times*, Sept. 18, 1979; Retrieved Dec. 24, 2022, from https://www.nytimes.com/1979/09/18/archives/starrett-city-lone-concern-rent-crime-rate-is-low-starrett-citys.html.

Page 100: *Due to the racial quotas, Black applicants waited for apartments in Starrett City nearly eight times as long as white applicants*: Peter Hellman, "A Dilemma Grows in Brooklyn," *New York Magazine*, Oct 17, 1988.

Page 100: *By 1983 the development's 5,881 apartments were fully occupied and of the 6,000 families on its waiting list, 75% were minorities*: George W. Goodman, "For Starrett City, an Integration Test," *The New York Times*, Oct. 16, 1983; Retrieved Dec. 24, 2022, from https://www.nytimes.com/1983/10/16/realestate/for-starrett-city-an-integration-test.html.

Page 100: *In 1979 a group of Black families represented by the National Association for the Advancement of Colored People initiated a class-action suit against Starrett City and the maintenance of its quota system. In May 1984 it was settled that Starrett City would in-*

crease the number of apartments for minorities by 175: Ann Mariano, "Backers of Racial Quotas Gain Support for Appeal," *The Washington Post*, Mar. 19, 1988; Retrieved Dec. 24, 2022, from https://www.washingtonpost.com/archive/realestate/1988/03/19/backers-of-racial-quotas-gain-support-for-appeal/fd6b5d40-0191-4d37-be10-6723cd163efe/.

Page 100: *the ratio of non-Hispanic white to minority families soon changed from 65% to 35%*: Walter Goodman, "Dispute Over Quotas at Starrett City," *The New York Times*, Jul. 13, 1984; Retrieved Dec. 24, 2022, from https://www.nytimes.com/1984/07/13/nyregion/dispute-over-quotas-at-starrett-city-complex-mix-of-principle-and-politics.html.

Page 119: *I've been to the mountaintop ... I've seen the Promised Land. I may not get there with you. But I want you to know tonight, that we, as a people, will get to the Promised Land*: Martin Luther King Jr, "I've Been to the Mountaintop," April 3, 1968; Retrieved Aug. 14, 2022, from https://kinginstitute.stanford.edu/encyclopedia/ive-been-mountaintop.

Page 124: *I Ain't Marching Any More*: Phil Ochs, "I Ain't Marching Any More," *I Ain't Marching Any More* (Elektra, 1965).

Page 131: *the Ortoiroid people, who moved from South America into the Caribbean around 1000 BC, were the first to settle on Puerto Rico, according to some sources*: Irving Rouse, *The Tainos: Rise and Decline of the People Who Greeted Columbus* (Yale University Press, 1993).

Page 140: *The Crown Heights riots began on August 19, 1991, after a driver in the motorcade of the leader of the Chabad movement accidently struck two children of Guyanese immigrants with his car, killing one and severely injuring the other*: Lily Rothman, "Read TIME's Report on the Crown Heights Riots of 1991," *Time*, Aug. 19, 2015; https://time.com/3989495/crown-heights-riots-time-magazine-history/.

Page 140: *In its wake several Jews were seriously injured and one man was killed. A few weeks following the riot a non-Jewish man, who some believe had been mistaken for a Jew, was killed by a group of Black men*: Edward S. Shapiro, *Crown Heights: Blacks, Jews, and the 1991 Brooklyn Riot* (Brandeis University Press, 2006).

Page 142: *From the redwood forest to the Gulf Stream waters*: Woody Guthrie, "This Land Is Your Land" (1945).

Pages 147–8: *Puerto Rico, my heart's devotion, Let it sink back in the ocean...*: Lyrics by Stephen Sondheim, Music by Leonard Bernstein. "America," *West Side Story* (Metro-Goldwyn-Mayer Studios, 1961).

Page 151: Juan Vidal, "Spic-O-Rama: Where 'Spic' Comes From, And Where It's

Going," NPR, Mar. 3, 2015; Retrieved Aug. 14, 2022, from https://www.npr.org/sections/codeswitch/2015/03/03/388705810/spic-o-rama-where-spic-comes-from-and-where-its-going.

Page 153: Tom Brokaw on NBC's *Meet the Press*, Jan. 27, 2019; Retrieved Aug. 14, 2022, from https://www.cnn.com/videos/media/2019/01/28/tom-brokaw-hispan-ics-should-work-harder-at-assimilation-sot-vpx.cnn.

Page 155: *A woman's place is right there now in her home*: Ray Charles, "I've Got a Woman," (Atlantic Records, 1954).

Page 156: *In an analysis conducted by the Pew Research Center in 2013...*: Jens Manuel Krogstad and Mark Hugo Lopez, "Use of Spanish declines among Latinos in major U.S. metros," Pew Research Center, Oct. 31, 2017; Retrieved Dec. 24, 2022, from https://www.pewresearch.org/fact-tank/2017/10/31/use-of-spanish-declines-among-latinos-in-major-u-s-metros/.

Page 157: *The first Puerto Rican baseball player to appear in the major leagues was a pitcher named Hiram Bithorn in 1942, whose actual last name was Sosa and of whom no one has ever heard of outside of Puerto Rico*: Andrew Kivette, National Baseball Hall of Fame and Museum; Retrieved Dec. 24, 2022, from https://baseballhall.org/discover/hiram-bithorn-debut.

Page 158: *Congress approved the Jones-Shafroth Act in 1917...*: "A Latinx Resource Guide: Civil Rights Cases and Events in the United States," Library of Congress; Retrieved Dec. 24, 2022, from https://guides.loc.gov/latinx-civil-rights/jones-shafroth-act.

Page 158: *One such WWI soldier was a man named Rafael Hernández Marín...*: Khaled Maalouf, "#VeteranOfTheDay Army Veteran Rafael Hernandez," *VA News*, Oct. 19, 2022; Retrieved Dec. 24, 2022, from https://news.va.gov/110066/veteranoftheday-army-rafael-hernandez/.

Page 159: *Don't look so sad, I know it's over... Lay your head upon my pillow*: Kris Krist-offerson. "For the Good Times," *Kristofferson* (Monument, 1970).

Page 169: *first seen in print*: Vidal, NPR.

Page 169: *spicks*: Ernest Peixotto, "Along the Mexican Border," *Scribner's Magazine*, Vol. LIX, Jan.–Jun., 1916.

Page 169: *He's a spic!*: F. Scott Fitzgerald, *Tender Is the Night* (Charles Scribner's Sons, 1934).

Page 174: *There's no there there*: Gertrude Stein, *Everybody's Autobiography* (Random House, 1937).

Page 175: *I have sinned, Lord, but I have several excellent excuses*: Spoken by Henry Fonda in the role of Pierre Bezukhov. *War and Peace* (Paramount Pictures, 1956).

Page 175: *Stories are like icebergs*: Ernest Hemingway's theory was explained in *Death in the Afternoon* (Charles Scribner's Sons, 1932): "If a writer of prose knows enough of what he is writing about he may omit things… The dignity of movement of an ice-berg is due to only one-eighth of it being above water."

Page 176: *You know how to whistle, don't you, Steve?*: Spoken by Lauren Bacall in the role of Marie "Slim" Browning. *To Have and Have Not* (Warner Bros., 1944).

Page 181: *Democracy Dies in Darkness*: *The Washington Post* added this slogan under its online masthead on Feb. 22, 2017.

Page 197: *Don't die before you're dead*: Yevgeny Yevtushenko, *Don't Die Before You're Dead* (Random House, 1995).

Page 206: *The Jewish Daily Bulletin report on July 28, 1926, had an "advance guard of the Porto Rican army" that planned to attack the Jews with long sticks and bricks*: "Riot Between Porto Ricans and Jews in Harlem is Prevented by the Police," *Jewish Telegraphic Agency*, July 28, 1926; Retrieved Dec. 24, 2022, from https://www.jta.org/archive/riot-between-porto-ricans-and-jews-in-harlem-is-prevented-by-the-police.

Page 207: *The Herald was staunchly anti-immigrant. The publisher, James Gordon Bennett Sr., reportedly said a newspaper's role is not to instruct, but to startle*: Katherine Roeder, *Wide Awake in Slumberland: Fantasy, Mass Culture, and Modernism in the Art of Winsor McCay* (University Press of Mississippi, 2014).

Page 212: *According to two Pew Research Center national surveys, researchers found that about half of second-generation self-identified Latinos are bilingual…*: Mark Hugo Lopez, Ana Gonzalez-Barrera, and Gustavo López, "Hispanic Identity Fades Across Generations as Immigrant Connections Fall Away," Pew Research Center, Dec. 20, 2017; Retrieved Dec. 24, 2022, from https://www.pewresearch.org/hispanic/2017/12/20/hispanic-identity-fades-across-generations-as-immigrant-connections-fall-away/.

Page 212: *What might've been lost don't bother me*: Bon Iver, "The Wolves (Act I and II)," *For Emma, Forever Ago* (Jagjaguwar, 2008).

Page 214–215: Esmeralda Santiago, *When I was Puerto Rican* (Cambridge: Da Capo Press, 2006).

Page 216: *According to the 2010 census, New York has the highest population of Puerto Rican residents, followed by Florida and New Jersey*: Sharon R. Ennis, Merarys Ríos-Vargas, and Nora G. Albert, "The Hispanic Population: 2010, Issued May 2011; Retrieved Dec. 24, 2022, from https://www.census.gov/content/dam/Census/library/publications/2011/dec/c2010br-04.pdf.

Page 217: *"I Don't Think the Cop is My Friend" is the title*...: "'I Don't Think the Cop Is My Friend,'" *The New York Times*, March 29, 1964; Retrieved Dec. 24, 2022, from https://www.nytimes.com/1964/03/29/archives/i-dont-think-the-cop-is-my-friend-so-say-many-of-new-years-puerto.html.

Page 217: *another young Puerto Rican named Francisco Rodriguez Jr. was shot dead by an off-duty policeman*...: "Rodriguez Youth Is Mourned by 300; Marchers Protest Shooting by Off-Duty Policema," *The New York Times*, Feb. 25, 1964; Retrieved Dec. 24, 2022, from https://www.nytimes.com/1964/02/25/archives/rodriguez-youth-is-mourned-by-300-marchers-protest-shooting-by.html.

Page 218: A *Puerto Rican lawyer said at the time, "Even though we come here as American citizens, many policemen look on us as aliens."*: "'I Don't Think the Cop Is My Friend,'" *The New York Times*, March 29, 1964.

Page 223: *The expression that there is nothing to express, nothing with which to express, nothing from which to express, no power to express, no desire to express, together with the obligation to express*: Samuel Beckett, "Three Dialogues," Disjecta: Miscellaneous writings and a dramatic fragment (Grove Press, 1984).

Page 223: *Who's gonna protect me from you? The likes of you? The nerve of you?*: Gil Scott-Heron, "No Knock," *Free Will* (Flying Dutchman Records,1972).

Page 224: *And there I was, sandwiched between Rita Dove and Rochita Loenen-Ruiz*: Roxane Gay, "We Are Many, We Are Everywhere," *The Rumpus*, Aug. 3, 2012; Retrieved Dec. 24, 2022, from https://therumpus.net/2012/08/03/we-are-many-we-are-everywhere/.

Page 226: *Everybody has got to die, but I have always believed an exception would be made in my case*: "From the Archives: Death Makes No Exception of Writer William Saroyan," *The Los Angeles Times*, May 19, 1981; Retrieved Dec. 24, 2022, from https://www.latimes.com/local/obituaries/archives/la-me-william-saroyan-19810519-story.html.

Page 226: *You can get killed just for living in your American skin*: Bruce Springsteen, "American Skin (41 Shots)," *High Hopes* (Columbia Records, 2001).

Page 226: *Sit still... til they remember how your boy was killed:* Patricia Smith, "Black, Poured Directly into the Wound," *The Golden Shovel Anthology: New Poems Honoring Gwendolyn Brooks* (University of Arkansas Press, 2019).

Page 228: *And we turn him into an anecdote to dine out on*...: John Guare, *Six Degrees of Separation: A Play* (Vintage Books, 1990).

Page 244: *Nobody beats Vitas Gerulaitis 17 times in a row*: Vitas Gerulaitis, "Tennis-Nobody beats Shelby Rogers six times in a row," *Reuters*, Sept. 5, 2021; Retrieved Dec. 24, 2022, from https://www.reuters.com/article/us-tennis-usopen-rogers-idCAKBN2G102W.

Page 252: *The region's provisional government passed a law excluding Black people from the territory in 1844*: DeNeen L. Brown, "When Portland banned blacks," *The Washington Post*, Jun. 7, 2017; Retrieved Dec. 24, 2022, from https://www.washingtonpost.com/news/retropolis/wp/2017/06/07/when-portland-banned-blacks-oregons-shameful-history-as-an-all-white-state/.

Page 252: *In the 1920s, Oregon had the largest chapter of the Ku Klux Klan west of the Mississippi*: Ben Bruce, "The Rise and Fall of The Ku Klux Klan in Oregon During the 1920s," *Voces Novae*: Vol. 11, Article 2. (2019); Retrieved Dec. 24, 2022, from https://digitalcommons.chapman.edu/cgi/viewcontent.cgi?article=1126&context=vocesnovae.

Page 252: *Oregon didn't re-ratify the 14th Amendment, adopted in 1868, which guaranteed equal protection of the laws and citizenship to all born or naturalized in the United States, including former enslaved people, until 1973*: "Black History Context (Later Developments)," The Oregon Secretary of State; Retrieved Dec. 24, 2022, from https://sos.oregon.gov/archives/exhibits/black-history/Pages/context/later-developments.aspx.

Page 252: *The obsolete language from the old law excluding Black people from Oregon wasn't removed from the state constitution until 2002. Even then, over a quarter of voters cast their ballot against the removal*: Tiffany Camhi, "A racist history shows why Oregon is still so white," Oregon Public Broadcasting, Jun. 9, 2020; Retrieved Dec. 24, 2022, from https://www.opb.org/news/article/oregon-white-history-racist-foundations-black-exclusion-laws/.

Page 252–3: *According to the 2010 U.S. census, less than 2% of Utah's population is Black, less than 3% Asian. Latinos/Latinas, which the U.S. government still refers to as Hispanics, comprise almost 13% of the population*: U.S. Census Bureau, August 25, 2021; Retrieved Dec. 24, 2022, from https://www.census.gov/library/stories/state-by-state/utah-population-change-between-census-decade.html.

Page 241: *It's just a fact of life that no one cares to mention, she wasn't good but she had good intentions*: Lyle Lovett, "Good Intentions," *Lyle Lovett and His Large Band* (Curb Records/MCA Records, 1989).

Page 254: *Democrats... don't care about crime and want illegal immigrants, no matter how bad they may be, to pour into and infest our country*: Betsy Klein and Kevin Liptak, "Trump ramps up rhetoric: Dems want 'illegal immigrants' to 'infest our country,'" CNN, Jun. 19, 2018; Retrieved Dec. 24, 2022, from https://www.cnn.com/2018/06/19/politics/trump-illegal-immigrants-infest/index.html.

Page 254: *is a disgusting, rat and rodent infested mess*: Ron Cassie, "Baltimore City Takes on Trump after President's Vitriolic Attacks," *Baltimore Magazine*, Jul. 28, 2019; Retrieved Dec. 24, 2022, from https://www.baltimoremagazine.com/section/community/wearebaltimore-city-takes-on-trump-after-presidents-vitriolic-attacks/.

Page 254: *instructed four Congresswomen to go back and help fix the totally broken and crime infested places from which they came*: Amelia Lucas, "Trump tells progressive congresswomen to 'go back' to where they came from," CNBC, Jul. 14 2019; Retrieved Dec. 24, 2022, from https://www.cnbc.com/2019/07/14/trump-tells-progressive-congresswomen-to-go-back-to-where-they-came-from.html.

Page 254: *appeared unaware that Puerto Rico is part of the United States*: Stephanie Murray, "Biden: Does Trump know Puerto Ricans are U.S. citizens?" *Politico*, Jun. 4, 2019; Retrieved Dec. 24, 2022, from https://www.politico.com/story/2019/06/04/biden-trump-puerto-rico-1353540.

Page 254: *the island's "incompetent" and "corrupt" politicians "only take from USA" and that Puerto Rico would "continue to hurt our Farmers and States with these massive payments"*: Bailey Vogt (*The Washington Times*) "Donald Trump slams 'incompetent' Puerto Rican politicians after disaster relief bill fails," AP News, April 2, 2019; Retrieved Dec. 24, 2022, from https://apnews.com/article/f7060cd-5b43b52816244313fa4dd6648.

Page 254: *wanted to sell Puerto Rico after the hurricane*: Michael D. Shear, "Leading Homeland Security Under a President Who Embraces 'Hate-Filled' Talk," *The New York Times*, Jul. 10, 2020; Retrieved Dec. 24, 2022, from https://www.nytimes.com/2020/07/10/us/politics/elaine-duke-homeland-security-trump.html?referringSource=articleShare.

Page 256: *Brigham Young was the one who marked its location in 1847... The site was dedicated on February 14, 1853*: "Background on the Salt Lake Temple," The Church of Jesus Christ of Latter-day Saints; Retrieved Dec. 24, 2022, from https://newsroom.churchofjesuschrist.org/additional-resources/background-on-the-salt-lake-temple.

Page 258: *It's immoral to let a sucker keep his money*: history of the quote attributed to Canada Bill Jones: Martin Harris, "Poker & Pop Culture: It's Immoral to Let a Sucker Keep His Money," *PokerNews*, Aug. 9, 2016; Retrieved Dec. 24, 2022, from https://www.pokernews.com/news/2016/08/poker-pop-culture-015-immoral-to-let-a-sucker-keep-his-money-25520.htm.

ROBERT LOPEZ is the author of three novels, *Part of the World*, *Kamby Bolongo Mean River*, named one of 25 important books of the decade by *HTML Giant*, and *All Back Full*; two story collections, *Asunder* and *Good People*, and a novel-in-stories titled *A Better Class of People*. His fiction, nonfiction, and poetry has appeared in dozens of publications, including *Bomb, The Threepenny Review, Vice Magazine, New England Review, The Sun*, and the *Norton Anthology of Sudden Fiction – Latino*. He teaches at Stony Brook University and has previously taught at Columbia University, The New School, Pratt Institute, and Syracuse University. He lives in Brooklyn, New York.